DRAGONS' DEN
DEN

START YOUR
OWN BUSINESS

DRAGONS' DEN

START YOUR OWN BUSINESS

FROM IDEA TO INCOME

RUS SLATER

Collins

A division of HarperCollins*Publishers*
77-85 Fulham Palace Road, London W6 8JB
First published in Great Britain in 2010 by HarperCollins*Publishers*
1
Copyright © HarperCollins*Publishers* 2010
Rus Slater asserts the moral right to be identified as the author of this work.

Foreword copyright © Evan Davis 2010

A catalogue record for this book is available from the British Library.
ISBN 978-0-00-736428-2

Dragons' Den

Created by Nippon Television Network Corporation
This book is produced under licence from 2waytraffic, a Sony Pictures Entertainment
company/CPT Holdings. Dragons' Den and all associated logos, images and trade marks
are owned and controlled by 2waytraffic.

Produced by Thameside Media
www.thamesidemedia.com

Printed and bound by Graficas Estella, Spain

Mixed Sources
Product group from well-managed
forests and other controlled sources
www.fsc.org   Cert no. SW-COC-001806
© 1996 Forest Stewardship Council

FSC is a non-profit international organisation established to promote the
responsible management of the world's forests. Products carrying the FSC
label are independently certified to assure consumers that they come
from forests that are managed to meet the social, economic and
ecological needs of present and future generations.

Find out more about HarperCollins and the environment at
www.harpercollins.co.uk/green

ABOUT THE AUTHOR

Rus Slater is a management consultant and trainer who has worked in many areas of industry, commerce and public service. He is the author of *Getting Things Done*, *People Management* and *Team Management* in the Business Secrets series, also published by HarperCollins.

CONTENTS

FOREWORD
FROM DRAGONS' DEN HOST
EVAN DAVIS

If you are a real entrepreneur, you probably don't have much time for books. You are probably supremely action-oriented and think that you learn more by doing rather than reading.

I have some sympathy with your view. If you were thinking of playing ice hockey for the first time or riding a motorbike, you would get nowhere without having an actual go. To paraphrase that well-worn saying, a single minute of experience is worth a thousand words.

But if you are a real entrepreneur please do read on. You probably need this book. In business – just as in ice hockey and motorcycling – mistakes are painful. Books can do a little to help you avoid them. They are not a substitute for action but an important supplement. And for those of you starting out in business, this book in particular is an invaluable aid.

What you will see here is a guide to the two layers of decision-making you face in a young company. At one level, there is the gritty detail: company annual returns, VAT and all that. At the other level, there is the big picture: the vision and mission, the product and marketing. Many people naturally incline to one or the other, but as an entrepreneur you must handle both. You can't afford to be just a detail person. You have to be able to look ahead to the horizon as well as at the ground in front of you.

But nor can you afford to be just a visionary. You can have as many big ideas as you like, you will get nowhere with them if you are caught in any of the legal and financial traps that are waiting to ensnare you.

Entrepreneurs can't afford to specialize. They don't have teams of people to take over the minor chores for them or to sit in a research department engaging in blue-sky thinking. It's all down to them, which is why entrepreneurs should recognize that some well-chosen reading material can help them out.

The best entrepreneurs have an uncanny knack of handling the little things without losing sight of the big. Many excellent examples have passed through the Dragons' Den and are featured in these pages. I hope you can learn from their stories and from the other people's experience which is contained in this volume. Don't let it go to waste.

Evan Davis

MAKE
A SOUND
DECISION

Are you sure you want
to start your own business?

INSPIRED BY DRAGONS' DEN? This book will help you as a budding entrepreneur to start up your own business. It will show you what to consider in terms of your business idea itself, your formal business plan, finance, marketing and sales. It will guide you through the red tape of starting a business in the UK. It will also ask questions of *you*, the brains behind your future business empire, so that you can coach yourself through the tricky start-up stages. Indeed, the very first question you must address right away is whether you *really* do want to start your own business. Are you actually suited to the entrepreneurial way of life? Whether you're not sure yet, or even if you think you're already sure, read your way through the whole book before making too many decisions!

Starting a business is not an action to be undertaken lightly. The average worker spends about 30% of their time at work. But if you start running your own business, your time at work will increase… a lot. You need to do some serious thinking and make sound decisions. When you are an employee, someone else takes the responsibility for ensuring that you have work to do, making sure that there is money in the bank to pay you – even when you are sick or injured – and that if you survive to retirement age you will get a pension. If you run your own business you have to take all this extra responsibility yourself.

On the one hand, if you have a 'proper job' and you mess up, you could be sacked. On the other hand, if you run your own business and mess up, you could lose everything.

SHARON WRIGHT OF MAGNAMOLE
(Episode 2, Series 7, see p41) described her fledgling business as her full-time job, weekend job and evening job.

WHAT'S YOUR MOTIVATION?

Starting your own business is the dream of many people and it is a legitimate desire in most cases. But before you go too far down the road of planning you should understand your own motivations for wanting to start up in the first place. When you make such a serious life decision as starting your own business you need to be certain that you are doing it for the 'right' reasons.

" THERE ARE THREE REASONS FOR GOING TO WORK. ONE TO MAKE MONEY, TWO TO HAVE FUN AND THREE, DON'T FORGET TO MAKE SOME MONEY. " THEO PAPHITIS, DRAGON

- **IS IT FOR THE MONEY?** Many budding entrepreneurs are motivated by the possibility of making more money than they do at present.

- **MORE FREEDOM OVER TIME.** You might be longing to work different hours rather than those set by your current boss.

- **FED UP WITH APPLYING FOR JOBS.** Updating your CV and going for interviews can be thankless and time-consuming. Perhaps you think your energies will be better focused on starting up a business.

- **A EUREKA MOMENT.** You've had an idea that could well be the Next Big Thing.

- **TURNING FUN INTO PROFIT.** You reckon your hobby could be a business earner.

- **AN INVESTMENT OPPORTUNITY.** You've had a redundancy settlement or inheritance that you want to invest, and you'd rather invest it in yourself than someone else.

Many people are motivated by one or more of these reasons to start up their own business. But there are pros and cons with each reason. Let's take a closer look at them.

1 **"I WANT TO TRY MAKING MORE MONEY FOR MYSELF"**

PROS: You get to pay yourself what you want. No one else profits from your work, just you. You get to be the boss.
CONS: You can pay yourself only what is surplus. You have to carry the can for any losses, which may mean losing everything. You may have to manage people and rely on and take responsibility for them.

2 **"I WANT TO SET MY OWN HOURS FOR WORKING"**

PROS: You can't be ticked off by a boss for being late. You don't have to ask to take time off. You can be flexible with your hours.
CONS: You will probably find that you have to work more hours than ever before. You have to be on time for your customers and clients. You won't get sick pay or holiday pay, and it may be difficult to find opportunities to take time off.

3 **"I'D RATHER GO SELF-EMPLOYED THAN GO FOR INTERVIEWS"**

PROS: You don't have to keep updating your CV, filling in application forms and going for interviews. There are often more short-term opportunities for self-employed people than 'proper' jobs around.
CONS: You will have to create marketing material and a

website. You are going to have to constantly sell yourself and your product or service.

4 "I'D LIKE TO TURN MY HOBBY INTO A BUSINESS"

PROS: You know you enjoy it.

CONS: There may not be enough people prepared to pay you to do it if it is that much fun! And will you still enjoy it when you have to do it in order to eat?

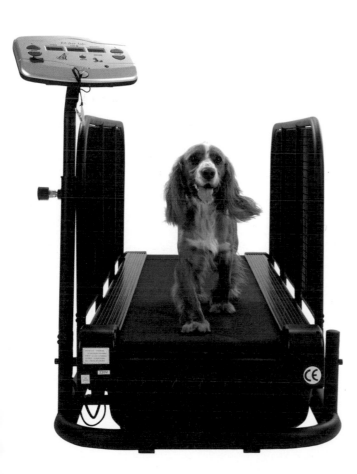

SAMMY FRENCH, *an entrepreneur from Series 5 of Dragons' Den (see p142), had spent her life breeding and training dogs. It was her passion and her intimate knowledge of their needs for training and rehabilitation that led to the creation of her business, producing specialist canine treadmills.*

5 "I'VE HAD A BRILLIANT IDEA THAT COULD WELL BE THE NEXT BIG THING"

PROS: Your idea might really take off.

CONS: Are you absolutely sure that it hasn't been done already? You're going to have to protect this idea from people who might copy it. And luck might be against you.

MAGIC PIZZA – *a metal disc that raises the centre of a pizza while it cooks – was the idea of Raymond Smith, who appeared in Dragons' Den Series 6. He had been disappointed by the soggy middles of the frozen pizzas he had been cooking. He worked to refine the invention, and on finding out the potential size of the market for this product he set about patenting it (see pp176–7). Though the Dragons weren't entirely convinced, Peter Jones was heard to exclaim: "This could be the cat's eyes of the pizza world!"*

6 "I'VE COME INTO SOME MONEY THAT I WANT TO INVEST IN MY OWN BUSINESS"

PROS: No one else is going to take a cut of the profits.

CONS: If you blow it you have only yourself to blame.

Think about whether you arc running *towards* being your own boss or running *away from* having a boss over you. This may seem a semantic difference but it is very important. Your current boss may be a drag to work for but does that mean you actually want to do all the things that boss does for you at the moment, such as ensure you get paid on time?

And have you actually got the Next Big Thing or are you simply convinced that the current way of doing things isn't working? Again, this may seem semantic, but it will probably be the difference between you having a real USP (unique selling point – see p39) or you being just another competitor offering the same thing: then it all becomes price sensitive!

THINK ABOUT THE PRACTICALITIES

The points so far have referred to your motivation in setting up your own business, and are pretty deep and philosophical. Once you have gone through this soul-searching, you need to become more practical. The likelihood of success depends on several important areas: the marketplace for your business; the overheads and operations required to bring the business into the marketplace; and your personal circumstances.

THE MARKETPLACE

- How much am I going to charge in relation to my needs (short and longer term) and the market (relative perception of the value of my product/service)?
- Why would someone buy my product or service rather than a competitor's?
- Why would anyone else want to invest in my venture?
- What is my target margin?
- How much profit do I need to make to stay afloat, and how quickly?
- How will I handle cash-flow needs?
- What is my route to market?
- Who are my competitors and what differentiates me from them?
- Where is the work/market geographically and does this suit my abilities and desires?

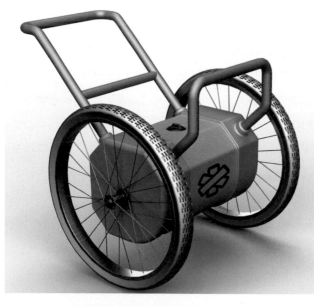

WITH RED BUTTON'S WATER CARRIER AND PURIFIER *(see opposite) the market was based on necessity rather than desire. As such, it would be bought not by the end users but by the charitable sector.*

RED BUTTON DESIGN

Red Button Design was founded by Amanda Jones and James Brown in 2007 with the aim of designing and manufacturing products that can be used as temporary solutions for acute humanitarian problems in the developing world. They show-cased a water transportation, purification and storage device for use as an interim measure in regions where access to clean drinking water is adversely affected.

AMANDA AND JAMES *made a confident pitch to the Dragons that equally explained their motivation and product.*

Their reasons for starting the business were two-fold: there were clear ongoing world problems that they wanted to help alleviate through the use of their analytical and technical design skills; and they saw how they could reinvest the profit from their products to continue finding further solutions to humanitarian problems. The income revenue would come not from the end users but from government aid packages and charities.

In their pitch Amanda and James appealed to the Dragons' philanthropic side, but also needed to prove their practical astuteness and financial criteria to secure funding from all five Dragons for a 2% stake each.

OPERATIONS AND OVERHEADS

- Am I able to and do I want to sell the service/product or will I have to get someone else to do that for me?
- I may be able to do the actual work, but what about the administration, quoting, invoicing and credit control?
- Am I able to do all the management: handling staff, contractors, suppliers, and dealing with the tax office?
- What overheads must I incur and what can I do without?

YOUR PERSONAL CIRCUMSTANCES

- How will I cope financially and emotionally with the possible bad times?
- What will I do if I cannot cope alone with the really good times? Will I have to turn away opportunities as 'too big'?
- Am I going to get lonely without a group of work colleagues?
- How am I going to separate work from home time?
- How will I cope if I'm sick?
- Can I afford (not) to insure against illness or injury causing loss of income?
- How long is this going to be viable as a business for me? Is this going to pay for my retirement?
- Can I accept that sometimes I'm going to have to let people down?

Some of these questions link to later chapters of this book but they are all things you want to be thinking about at the start. If you don't think about them you had better hope that no one ever catches you out Dragons' Den-style by asking you a question that leaves you looking ignorant or naive!

CONSIDER YOUR FAMILY

Even if your business is going to be, or at least start off as, a one-person band, you need to consider the people in life that you rely on and who rely on you: your spouse or partner, your parents, perhaps, or your children. You need to ensure that your spouse or partner will support you (or at least not hinder you) in your venture.

MAX MCMURDO OF REESTORE *(see also pp88–9) decided to employ his partner as his office manager as the business expanded so that he could concentrate on the area of work where his talent lies: designing new items of furniture.*

If your spouse is going to take an active role in your business then you need to have a clear understanding of who is the decision maker on what, and that expectations and responsibilities are business critical and not open to personal considerations.

If your spouse is not taking an active role in the business then you need to be sure that you have support over things such as working hours, business investment of surplus funds (as opposed to holidays etc), holiday time, weekends and so on.

If you are going to be based at home (whether your base is for storage, office space, workshop or studio) there needs to be clarity of expectation about working time, interruptions, safety and ownership of supplies and materials. This may of course impinge on a family's social life – you are working in the 'office' and the kids come home from primary school with some friends for a play-date and create merry havoc around your workstation, rendering it impossible for you to concentrate or use the phone.

CONSIDER YOUR NEIGHBOURS AND LOCAL AUTHORITY

If you're planning to start up your business from home, check the conditions in your lease and with your Local Authority. Tenancy agreements often include clauses that prevent residences being used for business purposes. Even if you own your property you should check whether there are any restrictive covenants on the property that may prevent you from operating your business from home.

Many restrictive covenants in the UK were written a long time ago and are no longer really appropriate – for instance covenants preventing you hanging out washing on Sundays or keeping a caravan on the property. It's also worth bearing in mind that a

NEIL AND LAURA WESTWOOD STARTED THEIR MAGIC WHITEBOARD COMPANY *(see pp228–9)*
from a home office. The business grew very rapidly and soon they were having huge lorries turn up at their home for delivery or dispatch. It caused problems for neighbours trying to get to work by car, so the couple hastily moved the business into premises right by a haulage company.

restrictive covenant would only have a material effect if someone were prepared to enforce it through the court, which is expensive. However, if your covenant is with a Local Authority it is much more potent. If your business requires partial conversion to business use (for example, using the garage as a workshop, or the front room as a studio for yoga students), then seek permission from your Local Authority. You may need to pay business rates on the proportion of your property that will be converted.

If anything is going to be visible or audible to your neighbours (e.g. storing materials in your garden), it is always better to discuss your plans with your neighbours first rather than hoping that they won't start complaining later.

CAN YOU START UP ALONGSIDE THE 'DAY JOB'?

It is possible to set up and run a part-time business alongside another job. The 'day job' could be a full-time or part-time PAYE job, or a caring role such as housewife or househusband. Many people start a small-scale business as a way of supplementing their income or pension. Starting in this way reduces the personal risk of a business that doesn't take off according to plan.

An article in the *Daily Mail* in January 2009 reported that according to a survey almost half of stay-at-home mothers use the internet and emails to raise some extra cash. Of this significant army of supplemental earners, one in 20 is earning at least £200 a month from 'using a computer mouse at home' and 'six per cent reckon they could easily turn their home-based work into a full-time job'.

If you are planning to set up a business whilst maintaining an employed role you must check your contract of employment, because some employers write clauses to stop this. The ban may seem an unreasonable stipulation (and in some cases it

RACHEL WATKYN'S PACKAGING BUSINESS *developed from an existing small business she ran selling jewellery. Rachel realized that there was potential for a bigger business selling boxes and other packaging items (see opposite).*

clearly is), but if your business could be seen as being in competition with your employer's, or contradictory to it, then there is a clear conflict of interest that will undoubtedly create problems later on.

TINY BOX COMPANY

Rachel Watkyn had a business that sold jewellery and wanted to send it out in eco-friendly packaging. Sourcing this was harder than she had thought, and she found that many packaging manufacturers were unclear even about the difference between recyclable and recycled materials!

In trying to buy her boxes, Rachel had in effect done some valuable market research. Not only had she spotted a small gap in the packaging market, but she had also found out that her potential rivals were not promoting this side of their business with knowledge and confidence. It may have been a slim market gap, but Rachel could see the potential for a new business, called Tiny Box Company. The company's USP would be that all its products were to be eco-friendly, and Rachel foresaw the market for such items increasing, as growing numbers of environmentally conscious consumers demanded more recycled and eco-friendly packaging. It was this market opportunity that drove her decision to start this business, rather than the products themselves.

Bear in mind, too, that there is a school of thought that trying to offset the effect of failure by continuing in full-time employment could, in itself, contribute to the failure of a business. Your goals might easily be diffused, and you won't have the 'hunger' that might otherwise drive you to make your business succeed.

ARE YOU ACTUALLY AN INVENTOR RATHER THAN AN ENTREPRENEUR?

Dragons' Den often uncovers people who are inventors looking for someone in shining armour to help them make money from their 'brainchild'. Unfortunately, conceiving a child is easier than bringing one up! If your eyes glaze over while reading about the practicalities that we cover in this book, perhaps you need to ask yourself if you've really got the entrepreneurial streak, or if it's the act of inventing itself that sets your pulse racing. If so, recognize now that you may be

WHEN PETER NEATH AND IAN WORTON *made their pitch in Series 7 of Dragons' Den they gave a practical demonstration of their invention for grilling food without letting fat drip through the grill. They proved themselves as inventors, but didn't convince the Dragons that they really knew what to do with their product. Dragon Theo Paphitis advised them to license the technology to an existing manufacturer of ovens and barbecues.*

better off not starting a full-blown business, rather you should be focusing on selling the licence for your invention.

" RESEARCH IT. MAKE SURE YOU'VE GOT A REALLY, REALLY GOOD IDEA. BE CONVINCED ABOUT IT. THEN GET PASSIONATE – DON'T GET PASSIONATE TOO EARLY. AND THEN DO IT, DO IT, DO IT. " DEBORAH MEADEN, DRAGON

MAKING UP YOUR MIND

When you've thought carefully about the issues we have raised in this chapter, you may well decide that you aren't going to set up your own business after all. That isn't failure… it is a good result because you analysed a situation and decided to take the course of action that was most likely to result in success! In the case study on the next pages you'll see that Lawrence Webb and Frank Drewett made the decision to opt for a licensing deal with their product. The financial rewards may not be so great, but it allowed them to continue with their existing businesses and ventures rather then dedicate themselves to manufacturing and marketing the product.

However, if you're still hell-bent on starting your own business, having examined your motives, considered your own capacity to make a success of it and also thought about the impact of your intentions of those around you, then carry on reading this book!

LID LIFTER

Establishing a business from scratch is not always the best option, especially with an invention-based business that will require manufacture, distribution, retail and marketing.

Lawrence Webb and Frank Drewett went to the Den in Series 7, looking for investment and a business strategy to make the most of Frank's patent for a pedal-bin device that lifts the lids of wheelie bins.

Unusually for a pitch based on a patent, it had in fact been around for about 12 years. Over that period, the device had been manufactured and sold in small numbers, but neither Frank nor Lawrence had had time to push on the marketing.

FRANK DREWETT *making his pitch in the Den: Frank said that, while he had received serious interest from a DIY chain, he was not happy with the price point at which they had wanted to retail the product, and so he had walked away from the potential deal.*

Now Lawrence had decided it was time to be more serious about marketing and selling the product. It was an idea in need of some business input.

The Dragons could see it was a useful device, but its lacklustre track record required further questioning. Why were the duo not more committed to making a go of it? Dragon Peter Jones concluded that it was not a business, but was a great opportunity to buy a valuable patent, and he made a bid based on that fact.

THE LICENSING ROUTE

Peter's insight in the Den was instrumental to the way Frank and Lawrence proceeded. Rather than trying to create a new business involving production, marketing and sales, they licensed it to a third party in return for a flat royalty fee on each unit sold.

The Lid Lifter for wheelie bins is now manufactured in a slicker form and sold through major retailers in the UK. This arrangement works well for Lawrence and Frank. The profits generate a modest income without the need for time or financial input from the pair.

THE OPERATION OF THE LID LIFTER *was demonstrated using rope, plastic and a wood model (top). The fully developed product (bottom) is now manufactured and sold under licence in the UK.*

DESIGN YOUR BUSINESS

What exactly is your product or service?

EARLY IN THE PLANNING STAGE you must develop a clear idea of what your business does and what you hope to achieve from it. You should define your vision and the mission of your business (they are two different things). What is the 'unique selling point' (USP) of your business? If you don't already know these points, then this chapter will help you identify them. This stage of the planning process is about research, research, research. And it may come as a surprise, but part of your planning at this stage should include your exit strategy. What is your long-term goal for the business – will you want to sell it on? Your exit strategy will be shaped by the way you design your business, and vice versa.

In these modern days of constant change it is more important than ever to ensure that your business has a clear definition of what it is and where it is going. Why? Because it will help your decision-making on a daily as well as long-term basis. It will help your customers know what they can expect of you and what not to expect of you. And it will help your backers (if you have them) to know what is in it for them and what timeframes to expect it by.

There are two aspects to this definition:

- **KNOWING YOURSELF WHERE YOUR BUSINESS IS GOING.**
  In other words, what is your vision and what is the mission of the business?

- **TELLING OTHER PEOPLE WHAT YOUR BUSINESS DOES.**
  In other words, what is the USP of your business?

HAVE A VISION FOR YOUR BUSINESS

Although some businesspeople use the terms 'vision' and 'mission' interchangeably, they are treated separately in this book. The 'vision' is your long-term aspiration and it can be financially-driven, product-driven or customer-driven. For instance, are you planning the business primarily to provide you with a personal income for the period of your working life, or do you want a business with a sale value so that you can use the money to fund your next business or retirement? Do you want to continue doing what you enjoy (working with a specific product or service) or is your desire to become the head of an empire with other people doing the actual work?

A FINANCIALLY-DRIVEN VISION

Think back to the subject at the beginning of chapter one. If you want to start your own business primarily to make lots of money or to invest an inheritance, then that itself will form the basis of your vision. It will guide you into various areas of business with potential for lots of money, rather than targeting a specific product or service that's 'your thing'. Arthur (or more recently Archie) Daley, of TVs *Minder* is an example of this – his business goes wherever there is a nice little earner. In real life, the Virgin Group has similarities: transatlantic airline, train operator, music industry, satellite TV, cola, condoms…

TONY EARNSHAW OF UK COMMERCIAL CLEANING, *who appeared in Series 7 of Dragons' Den, had a crystal clear vision for the business: to be the biggest and best commercial cleaning company in the UK. It's a simple goal and a bold one – it leaves no room for doubt and sets a challenge for the company.*

A PRODUCT-DRIVEN VISION

Again thinking about your initial motivation – if you have invented, designed or discovered the 'Next Big Thing' – you may have a vision to deliver this to the world. Many of the hopefuls who appear in front of the Dragons fall into this category. Famous examples of product-driven visions include that of James Dyson, with his vacuum cleaner technology, and Trevor Bayliss, with his wind-up radio. A franchise is usually a product-driven business: McDonald's sells only MacDonald's products to the hungry; Black Horse Financial Services sells only Lloyds TSB products.

A CUSTOMER-DRIVEN VISION

If your initial motivation is 'Next Big Thing' in a service arena or if you want to be the boss because you are convinced that you can do it better than the bosses you've worked for, then your vision will be to provide the customer with the best (for the customer) product or service possible, regardless of the brand.

For example, an Independent Financial Advisor can sell the best pension or investment insurance, not just Lloyds TSB's best. A 'free house' can sell the beers their customers want rather than having to sell a particular brewery's output.

What you choose as your vision will have a significant impact on the way your business goes and the way you live your life.

TOBY AND OLIVER RICHMOND'S BUSINESS, SERVICING STOP, *which featured in Series 7, has a customer-driven vision. The brothers saw a gap in the car servicing market for being better value than the main dealerships, whilst offering to customers the guarantees associated with a UK-wide organization.*

CREATE A MISSION STATEMENT FOR YOUR BUSINESS

The 'mission' of your business follows on from your 'vision' and describes what the business actually does for customers on a daily basis. Many companies publish mission statements:

GOOGLE'S MISSION

- To organize the world's information and make it universally accessible and useful

VIRGIN ATLANTIC'S MISSION

- **MISSION ONE:** To grow a profitable airline
- **MISSION TWO:** Where people love to fly
- **MISSION THREE:** And where people love to work

Let's take a hypothetical example to see how the mission alters according to the type of activity taking place.

After quitting a high-pressure job in the city, Andy Jones wants to set up as a painter and decorator because he has always been quite good at it and enjoys the work. He wants to start his own business to do this rather than start at the bottom of someone else's company.

Andy should define the mission of his business. Would he be content with the idea of putting on two coats of magnolia regularly for the Local Authority and Housing Association? If so, his mission could be simply: *"To paint and decorate property to a high standard."*

A prospective customer finds Andy's business card on their doormat. This card makes it clear that he is a solo operator and his service is painting and decorating for local people:

If, however, Andy wants a more designer-orientated business – perhaps he is a dab hand at interior design and colour schemes, and/or he wants to provide a value-added service for more well-heeled customers – then he needs a different mission. His mission might be *"To create living spaces that customers love."* The designer emphasis is reflected in Andy's business card:

The mission of Andy's intended business also has an effect on the people Andy wants to approach for backing and business support. 'Andy Jones Painter and Decorator' is a relatively low-risk business with a reasonable chance of quick turnover and high volumes of work at a relatively low margin. 'Jones Interiors' will have a far slower turnaround of projects, potentially a higher margin but a greater risk of customer dissatisfaction. The two options would have very different client bases that may be geographically separated.

DEFINE YOUR UNIQUE SELLING POINT (USP)

Many businesses are simply clones of others. Consider, for example, the burger bar industry. There are many successful burger bars that are identical to others in other areas, so much so that the industry has recognized the value of a proven formula and franchised the design. Burger bars that are independent, however, are always facing the danger of being undercut by the competition.

If you consider any marketplace, there is usually room for some clones to compete and succeed simply because the market is big enough to support several businesses.

BASSTONESLAP *appeared in Series 7. Their drumming performances and team-building workshops clearly had verve and originality. It wasn't a unique business – though few in number, there were other drumming-based workshop businesses and that fact actually served as a market indicator when the group made their pitch for investment. They were able to point to similar franchises that had sold for £100,000, thereby indicating market potential and value in their kind of business.*

IN THE CASE OF MAGNAMOLE *(see opposite), there had never been a product like it on the market before. Prior to its invention, workers had just made do with improvised devices such as coat hangers and screwdrivers to hook or push cable through cavity walls.*

However, if there are too many clone businesses and the only real difference between them is price, this starts a price war. The clones undercut one another, which isn't sustainable, and so they start to go out of business. Failure at this point is not dependent on quality of product or service but other factors, such as how much borrowing a business is trying to service or how much pain its owners and staff are prepared to endure before they throw in the towel.

In order not to face this danger, a business needs to find and exploit its USP – Unique Selling Point. This is something that sets your product or service apart from your competitors in the eyes and minds of your prospective customers.

MAGNAMOLE

Sharon Wright went into the Dragons' Den in Series 7 with a product-driven business called Magnamole. Whilst watching a communications engineer grappling with a coat hanger in order to thread cable through the cavity walls in her new home, she had 'a eureka moment' and thought of a simple device that would do the job quickly, safely and cheaply.

Her invention was a plastic rod, rigid enough to follow the drill holes, with a magnetic end so that cable could be attached to it (via a detachable clip) and

THE MAGNAMOLE KIT, *packaged for retail.*

simply pushed through the wall. Convinced that this was a great product for solving a very common but largely overlooked problem, Sharon developed a prototype and then went about marketing and selling Magnamole to the major DIY and cable installation companies in the UK. She also began the process of obtaining a worldwide patent for her invention – an important consideration for any product-driven business. Her pitch was one of the most accomplished ever seen in the Den.

In a crowded market, if you don't have a USP then your business could easily end up as just another 'also ran'. Your prospective customers will tend to compare your offering with others purely on price. You will have no clear competitive edge, and there will be no outstanding reason for people to consider buying from you.

HOW DO YOU FIND YOUR USP?

To continue the burger bar analogy, the USP of a burger bar may be its flame-grilled aspect, its mascot, its décor, its family history or its quality. Now think about your own business. You must identify what singles you out from the competition. To start you off, try a description from something like "the only..." or "no-one else can..."

PART OF YOUR USP, OR EVEN ITS ENTIRETY, MIGHT EVEN BE YOU YOURSELF!
You don't have to be a famous personality for this to be the case, but you do have to be highly charismatic. Think of Laban Roomes, who appeared in Series 5 of Dragons' Den. He had poise, determination and a bit of swagger – characteristics that were great for leading his gold-plating business, Goldgenie (see pp154–5).

> **" KNOWING, BELIEVING AND UNDERSTANDING YOUR PRODUCT OR SERVICE IS PARAMOUNT. AN IDEA, EVEN A GOOD ONE, WILL NOT TAKE OFF BY ITSELF. EXECUTION IS CRITICAL. "**
>
> JAMES CAAN, DRAGON

For example:
- "The only local supplier of ..."
- "The exclusive supplier to the ... industry"
- "Sole Agent for ..."
- "Voted Britain's best/favourite ..."
- "Inventor of the ..."

Think of businesses that proclaim their Royal Warrant: "By appointment to Her Majesty." Okay, so you can't make something up that isn't true, but you should be able to find some angle.

Look to cultural references for inspiration. For example, remember in the film *The Dambusters* when Barnes Wallis is trying to persuade the Air Ministry to let him have a Wellington Bomber and they ask why they should trust him and he says: "Because I invented it!"

Don't kid yourself that "we offer good service" or "I'm friendly" will be adequate. The only way a customer can check these claims is to pay you to provide the service, so that won't work. Besides which, all your competitors can make the same claim, so a statement on those lines wouldn't be a Unique Selling Point.

If you are already extremely successful or a well-known personality, then you may be the USP of your business. Successful sports personalities who go into motivational speaking or business coaching are able simply to put their names as their USP – look at Will Carling when he set up Insights Ltd or the plethora of well-known champions who are the USPs of Raise the Bar, for example.

Otherwise you might have a USP based on where you trained. The credentials of the Beyond Fear team are a good example of this: "Trained to withstand the most gruelling training regime, the SAS produces the world's most skilled soldiers with a reputation for their sophistication in tactical assault, precision pararescue skills and overall relentless endurance. Rick heads the Perth team of ex-SAS soldiers."

To conclude, if you have a good, clear (and honest) USP, there is a high chance that you will be able to compete on factors other than price. This prevents you from being forced into a price-cutting war with your competitors and allows you to maintain a more equitable profit margin.

However, in order to assess whether your USP is actually unique, you are going to have to do some serious market research…

RESEARCH THE MARKET

To strip away the jargon, market research is the collection and analysis of information about markets, organizations and people to support better business decisions.

Market research is vital for new businesses seeking a commercial opportunity. From identifying or confirming a gap in the market through to helping you establish an appropriate pricing structure, decent research can provide the market intelligence needed to improve your likelihood of success and therefore reduce the risk of loss, either of face or funds!

You can use a variety of research techniques, depending on the kind of information that you need and the budget that is available to you:

IN MICHAEL COTTON'S PITCH *in Series 6, he used facts to build a powerful case for his device that prevents incorrectly fuelling a car. He told the Dragons that this problem happens about 150,000–200,000 times a year in the UK, causing terrible engine damage. He also stated that the market for diesel vehicles in Europe is 78 million, 11 million in the UK alone. It gave a vivid impression of the scope of the business.*

- **NUMERICAL DATA** can be gathered in face-to-face interviews and through surveys using the Internet, the telephone or even by post.

- **QUALITATIVE RESEARCH**, questioning people about why they hold certain views, yields a greater understanding of customers than numerical data.

Market research has an important role in many business situations. It can help you identify the following:

- **EVIDENCE** of an existing market for your proposed product or service
- **SIZE** of the market
- **PRICING** that the market can support
- **COMPETITORS** and levels of customer loyalty to them
- **ALTERNATIVE PRODUCTS OR SERVICES** wanted by the market, which you may not have considered

Market research can also be used to test the desire for new products or services without massive risk.

The amount of data you need to collect and the time that will take will vary depending on the business you are aiming to start. A high street hairdressing salon or coffee shop will probably need less research than a local landscaping business, which in turn will be less exacting than a business that aims to sell nationally from day one.

Similarly, the actual amount you intend to invest in the business as a whole will determine how much research you want to do. A £5k start-up won't justify a 20-week market research programme, whilst a £200,000 investment merits more than a chat with some potential punters in the pub. If your budget is closer to the latter, then you should get a copy of the *Research Buyers Guide* from the Market Research Society (www.rbg.org.uk) and seriously consider employing professionals to help you.

Whether doing your own research or commissioning a professional firm, you need to be clear about what information you need to collect. There are several commonly recommended areas, covered on the next few pages.

WHO ELSE IS DOING WHAT YOU PROPOSE TO DO IN THE AREA?

For some forms of business, finding out who else is trading could be as simple as walking down the high street or checking the local business directories and online. Your Local Authority knows who is paying business rates and may be able to give you listings.

Businesses that are less visible to the consumer, e.g. manufacturing and business-to-business services, might be harder to identify, but trade organizations could be a first port of call for listings.

ANDY HARSLEY'S RAPSTRAP INVENTION *(see pp196–7) stepped into a market in which there were already several types of cable tie. Andy was sure, though, that for most uses of this kind of product, his version was better and more economical. Conventional hard plastic ties were stronger, but for the majority of uses the strength was superfluous. Andy's Rapstrap could be cut to length and reused, making it more versatile.*

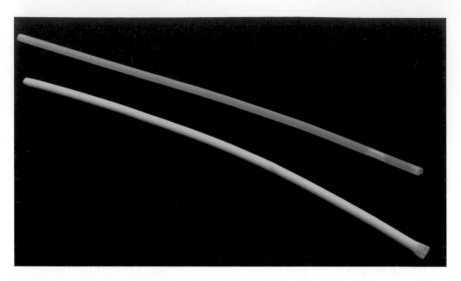

MICHAEL PRITCHARD'S INVENTION, THE ANYWAY SPRAY *(see also p165), presented a similar case to Andy Harsley's (see previous page). Dip tubes for aerosols and other sprays already existed. Michael's version was much better though and even worked upside down. This would be a benefit to the end user, but Michael proposed a licensing deal with manufacturers of such sprays. It was a good plan, but the hurdle would be convincing those manufacturers that it would be worth their while changing to the new dip tube.*

Your bank manager may have information on the number of businesses operating in your sector, along with other useful information, such as average turnover.

If your intended business is truly innovative and seemingly there is no one in the market at the moment, you must also question why not. At this stage you need to test the waters by questioning target customers whether they need such a product, and if so how much they need it and how much they would be prepared to buy and to pay.

HOW DO YOU FIND THE DETAILS OF THEIR SERVICES/PRODUCTS?

Again this will depend on the type of business. You can look in through the window of high street businesses and see their style, décor, prices and clientèle. With most other businesses you are somewhat more reliant on looking at their advertising or speaking to their customers. You can also engage in mild subterfuge – contact them as a prospective customer and ask for a quote… This will tell you a lot about their approach, professionalism and prices.

You can look at any UK company's profile on the Companies House website (www.companieshouse.gov.uk) and order information about them, including, for a very small fee, their annual accounts!

If you haven't found evidence of anyone working in your proposed market, look harder… remember that "absence of evidence isn't evidence of absence".

HOW DOES THE COMPETITION AFFECT YOUR USP?

If the market is totally saturated with suppliers, you will have to find a truly amazing USP to gain even the most minute market share!

WHAT PRICES ARE THEY CHARGING?

Knowing the average price and range of prices being sustained in the market will give you an initial idea of your own possible pricing structure. In line with your USP and your mission you can decide whether you are competing on price, pricing in the norm and competing on your USP, or going for a 'premium product and pricing' strategy.

WHICH OF THEM IS THE BEST?

'Best' can be judged according to your own criteria. If you are opening a bankrupt stock shop then 'best' might simply mean cheapest. If you are starting a swimming pool installation business, 'best' will probably relate to quality and service. If you are starting up an eBay-based trading shop, 'best' will probably be based on a combination of items sold and feedback scores. Everything is subjective – if you are intending to trade out of your spare room as a supplemental earner in your retirement you probably won't want to be comparing yourself to a full-time, staffed trader with 100,000 sales per year!

Once the research has been completed, you should make time to analyse it and draw logical conclusions. Put aside your ego here and listen to the 'Voice of the Customer'. If the research suggests strongly that your business idea will crash and burn, than be prepared to walk away from that business idea. Market research does not itself guarantee business success. Rather, the greater knowledge you have, the better equipped you will be to make a positive start.

PLAN YOUR EXIT STRATEGY FROM DAY ONE

Strange though it may sound in a book about starting your own business, you should also formulate your 'exit strategy' at an early stage of planning.

Although official figures are hard to obtain, it is said that more than half of all start-ups cease trading within two to four years. In 2009 there were 19,278 UK companies that officially went bust – i.e. they were logged either as creditors' voluntary liquidations or compulsory liquidations. From this statistic alone, you can see that you need to go into business with your eyes wide open to the possibility of failure and so plan your exit route accordingly.

WHEN HELEN WOOLDRIDGE AND POLLY MARSH OF CUDDLEDRY *appeared in the Den in Series 5, they seemed focused more on the product (towels designed for babies) than the business. If that were the case, success has changed their attitude: they have grown as a company and expanded their market presence internationally, and their plans are now geared towards selling the business in year six to finance a new entrepreneurial venture.*

Then again, let's say your business is successful. Are you planning it as a way to provide you with an income throughout your life, or do you view it as a saleable commodity that could fund your next business or your retirement? Your answer to this question also helps you understand the need for an exit strategy.

The exit strategy is predominantly aimed to help you exit your money from the business, but it can also relate to exiting you from the business as well.

WHAT MIGHT HAPPEN IF YOU DON'T HAVE AN EXIT STRATEGY

Here's a cautionary tale. A fellow sets up in business as a roofer, works successfully for 25 years and bags pretty much all the best contracts in his area and loyal repeat business in the trade. He employs three men on a permanent basis. Everyone is satisfied.

On reaching retirement age, the roofer puts the business up for sale, expecting to get about £100,000 based on the profitability of the business. But no one buys it. The roofer's love of his work has kept him at the forefront, while his employees have been almost invisible. Without him, therefore, the business has no value.

The roofer eventually sells the business to his employees for a nominal figure, but it folds soon afterwards because the customers assume that the original owner's retirement was the end of the firm. The roofer lost his anticipated nest egg, his employees lost their livelihoods and the customers lost a good supplier. All for the want of an exit strategy!

THE MAIN EXIT STRATEGIES FOR ENTREPRENEURS

STRATEGY – MILKING A LIFESTYLE BUSINESS

A 'lifestyle company' is one where the objective of the company is solely to provide a lifestyle for the owners; there is no intention to expand, diversify or employ others. A management trainer who doesn't employ anyone else is an example. Ditto a self-employed plumber or web designer. The business could operate as a Sole Trader, Partnership or even a Limited Company. Other shareholders might be family members – a husband-and-wife team is fairly common.

" **IF SOMEONE WANTS A BUSINESS THAT CAN BE REPEATED, RATHER THAN JUST GIVES THEM AN INCOME, THEN THEY HAVE TO MAKE SURE IT'S A SCALEABLE BUSINESS. THAT'S A KEY ELEMENT MANY PEOPLE FORGET. IF, AS SOON AS YOU BRING SOMEONE IN TO HELP, IT ALL FALLS APART, THAT'S NOT A REAL BUSINESS TO ME, THAT'S A LIFESTYLE BUSINESS. "** THEO PAPHITIS, DRAGON

Maintaining a lifestyle company usually means you take the entire surplus, paying yourself the maximum possible. You avoid reinvesting money in growing the business, rather, you deliberately keep things small and simply live on the income.

Unfortunately, for many lifestyle companies there is no formal exit strategy. If you salt away lots in savings and pension funds, then that is a form of exit strategy, but many small business people enjoy

MICHAEL NORTH MADE AN ENTHUSIASTIC PLEA FOR INVESTMENT *in his olive oil club for discerning gourmets who would appreciate 'fresh, seasonal olive oil'. However, as the plan involved him travelling the world to taste and bring back oil to the club members, the Dragons found it difficult to see the venture as anything other than a lifestyle business. It would allow Michael to indulge his passion, make a decent living and proselytize on the wonders of olive oil, but it wasn't deemed a good investment prospect.*

the (relative) high life and then realize that their business is worthless without them; they ARE the business. The personal exit strategy might be to 'get a job', but the entrepreneur still has to have a plan for getting their money out of the lifestyle business… usually this is covered by 'milking it dry'.

If you think you're in business for the lifestyle, you must minimize your dependence on other investors from the start and structure the business to allow you to draw out cash as needed. (And don't go on Dragons' Den looking for a lump sum investment in return for a percentage of your business!)

EXIT STRATEGY – DISSOLVING THE BUSINESS

Who knows where you are going to be in 10 years time? Even the most driven of entrepreneurs may decide that enough is enough, either through personal circumstances (illness, divorce etc), having made a pile of money or just getting bored. One often-overlooked exit strategy is simply to pack up and call it a day. You wind up the business without trying to sell it, and move on to something else.

Liquidating a company means to sell off its assets (e.g. stock and equipment), pay outstanding debts, distribute the remaining funds to shareholders and then go out of business. If there are other shareholders in your company, you must make sure they get their due – what's left is yours.

A caveat on liquidation: intangible assets like client lists, your reputation, and your business relationships may actually be worth a lot more than your tangible assets. Liquidation just destroys them without an opportunity to benefit from their value.

Liquidating an insolvent company (one that cannot pay off all its debts through liquidation) is a situation that many failed businesses face and it can have long-term repercussions. Depending on how you finance your venture, you may not be able to walk away from all the company's debts, and you will probably destroy your business relationships with clients and creditors. Thus, planning to trade insolvent and then liquidate is NOT a valid 'exit strategy' – it would be regarded as fraud.

" **THE PERSON WHO STARTS A BUSINESS IS NOT NECESSARILY BEST SUITED TO TAKING IT FORWARD. WE ALL HAVE LIMITS, AND THE SIGN OF A GREAT LEADER OR CEO IS KNOWING WHEN THAT STAGE HAS ARRIVED. IT'S NOT FAILURE. IT'S AN INHERENT UNDERSTANDING OF ONE'S STRENGTHS AND WEAKNESSES. "** JAMES CAAN, DRAGON

EXIT STRATEGY – SELLING TO A FRIENDLY BUYER

Potentially easier and more lucrative than liquidating your business is the option of passing ownership to another 'true believer' who wants to keep the business going. People like this might include customers, employees, your children or other family members.

If the interested parties cannot afford to buy you out completely you can arrange a deal whereby you finance the sale and let the buyers pay it off over time. This way you still make more money than you would by closing down, and the buyers get to earn their way into owning a business. It's a win-win for everyone involved.

The purest friendly buyout would be to a family member. However, there are two major issues here. Firstly, do family members see this as an advance on their inheritance? In this case you might be virtually giving the business away, which is only okay if you can afford to. Secondly, are the family members agreed on responsibilities and returns? You don't want to be the cause of family squabbles in the future over who does what and who gets what. If you decide to go this route, you've got a lot of planning to do before getting out.

EXIT STRATEGY – SELLING TO AN ACQUISITIVE COMPANY

Here you really may be able to negotiate a price that is good for your interests. In an acquisition, the sky's potentially the limit on your perceived value: a competitor may value simply removing you from the market; a complementary acquirer may value the synergy far

LESLEY-ANN SIMMONS SOLD HER SHOES GALORE FRANCHISE BUSINESS *soon after entering the Den in Series 6, having reflected on Theo's advice about the financial pitfalls of overtrading. Money from the sale of the business gave her the opportunity to seek out a new entrepreneurial project.*

more than the value of your profitability alone. The people making the acquisition decision are rarely the actual owners of the acquiring company, so they don't personally feel the pain of the cost of acquisition. Convince them you're worth a lot, and they'll gladly break out their employer's chequebook.

One company, Bebo, was just 18 months old in 2006 when put up for sale at $1 billion. This huge price was asked for because Bebo's social networking capabilities at the time made it extremely valuable to the telecoms giants, and it was finally bought by AOL for $850 million. Yes, there are many tales of acquisitions that go bad after the deal is done (e.g. after two years AOL announced they were planning to sell or shut down Bebo), but that won't be your problem… you will have moved on with your pockets jingling!

EXIT STRATEGY – GOING FOR STOCK MARKET FLOTATION

Technically speaking this is an 'exit strategy', and if you can do it and if you can get it right then you will become a multi-millionaire and a household name. It is, however, a rare occurrence. Floating a company on the stock market is a long, technically complex and very expensive business. You are not only trying to woo individual buyers but an entire market. Whilst you might want to consider stock market flotation as an exit strategy, it certainly isn't an option that is going to be open to many entrepreneurs and it definitely requires some of that very expensive advice.

These first two chapters have helped you understand the 'big picture' of running a business. The next chapter will look at the technicalities of starting up a business in the UK today.

KCO ICEBLADING

Although inline skates have been around for many years, the KCO inline skate – known as the Dry Ice Blade – has a definite USP in that it is the UK's first and only inline skate to accurately mimic the feel and action of an ice skate when in use.

This ability enables a skater without access to an ice rink to practise all their skating moves, including jumps and turns, on a typical gym floor.

To bolster the strength of their product's USP prior to going on the Den in Series 7, KCO's founders, Karen O'Neill and Karen Coombes, obtained a letter of endorsement from the National Ice Skating Association (NISA) stating to the effect that their skate would be a useful training aid for ice skaters. In their pitch, the duo introduced the idea of three revenue streams (retail, education, and health and fitness). However, under questioning, they didn't express a clear business

THE DRY ICE BLADES *allow a slight rocking action that replicates the curved blade of an ice skate.*

plan to generate a profit-able business, and it was unclear how much each of these revenue streams would contribute. But that all-important USP in a potentially expanding market ultimately made their pitch successful, with Dragon Theo Paphitis eventually offering to invest.

Theo was impressed by the industry testimonials about the product and, with so much current interest in skating due to TV programmes such as 'Dancing on Ice', he saw a chance of success for the skate as a retail product. He decided to invest, albeit with a high stake (45%), reflecting how much input he felt he would need to put in to take the KCO Dry Ice Blade to market.

KAREN O'NEILL AND KAREN COOMBES *made a lively and energetic pitch, even leaping in the air to demonstrate the kind of skills that can be performed with their Dry Ice Blades.*

A LIVE DEMONSTRATION *of the skates in action showed the Dragons and TV audience how they could be used on a simple wooden floor.*

ADDRESS THE FORMALITIES

Are you ready to acquaint yourself with Her Majesty's Revenue & Customs?

RIGHT. YOU'VE GRASPED THE BIGGER PICTURE. You've done some soul-searching as to what's motivating you to start a business in the first place. You've created a vision and mission statement and identified the USP of your business. You've even developed an exit strategy. Now we're going to explain the formal side of running a business in the UK today. It may be tedious to deal with red tape and tax issues, but you absolutely must understand the legal responsibilities you will have as the owner of a business. Did you know, for instance, that you will be slapped with a hefty fine if you're late in filing a company return? If you're not prepared to address the formalities, then just forget about starting up your own business.

THE RESPONSIBILITY *of running a business is not to be undertaken lightly. You need to understand the different business structures in the UK, along with tax obligations. Your signature on numerous documents will make you personally responsible for your business and the people related to it.*

YOUR LEGAL OBLIGATIONS

The laws governing business differ around the world, including within the countries of the European Union. In the UK, you have to make up your mind from the outset about what kind of formal structure, or legal entity, your business will take. This affects the way in which you are assessed for tax. You also have to comply with the UK's employment laws and standards of protection for consumers and the general public.

There are several areas you need to get to grips with, which are summarized in the points here. The rest of the chapter looks at each point in more detail.

- **WHAT WILL BE THE FORMAL STRUCTURE FOR THE BUSINESS?** Are you going to be self-employed as a Sole Trader, or do you need something more 'formal' such as a Partnership, Limited Company or Limited Liability Partnership? We look at the main types of business structure on pages 64–8.

- **WHAT ABOUT TAX?** Much of this will flow from the formal structure you choose. You will also need to make a decision regarding VAT registration. See pages 69–80.

- **WHAT OBLIGATIONS DO YOU HAVE TO YOUR STAFF?** Even casual workers have rights and bring responsibilities. On pages 80–83 we explain your obligations as an employer.

- **WHAT OBLIGATIONS DO YOU HAVE TOWARDS CUSTOMERS?** Depending on the way you trade and the type of business you are in, you may have more or less legal obligation to your customers. Many of these obligations can be covered by insurances but you must decide which ones you need. See pages 83–6.

- **WHAT OBLIGATIONS DO YOU HAVE TO THE PUBLIC AT LARGE?** Whilst some of these may be fairly obvious such as Health and Safety obligations, what about planning law in relation to your business address? See page 87.

" IT WAS AS TRUE – SAID MR BARKIS, NODDING HIS NIGHTCAP – AS TAXES IS. AND NOTHING'S TRUER THAN THEM. "

CHARLES DICKENS, FROM 'DAVID COPPERFIELD'

CHOOSE THE FORMAL VEHICLE FOR YOUR BUSINESS

There are three main types of business structure in the UK: **SOLE TRADER**, **PARTNERSHIP** and **LIMITED COMPANY**. Other structures include Social Enterprise and Charity, which are not covered in this book.

SOLE TRADER

This is the simplest business model to adopt. It simply means that you, as an individual, are engaging in business activities.

- **PROS OF SOLE TRADER:** As a Sole Trader you don't even have to set up a separate bank account for your small business activities, although it's usual to do so. As long as you keep records of your business income and expenses and record them properly on your tax return, there's little mandatory paperwork: you can just get on and start earning money. It just takes a simple form from the HMRC (www.hmrc.gov.uk), and you are officially a Sole Trader. You don't even have to use an accountant or solicitor if your accounts and contracts are simple.

" **ACTUALLY, STARTING A BUSINESS IS INCREDIBLY EASY – YOU COULD GO OUT TOMORROW, PRINT UP A LOAD OF BUSINESS CARDS, AND START – THE KEY IS MAKING THAT BUSINESS SUCCESSFUL AND SUSTAINABLE. "**

DEBORAH MEADEN, DRAGON

- **CONS OF SOLE TRADER:** You are the business. If you're sued by a customer or a member of the public or you fail to pay back a loan or overdraft, then you are personally liable and could lose everything. (Though you may be able to take out Professional Indemnity and Public Liability Insurances to offset some of these risks, see pp85–7.) You don't have a very strong image – potential customers and clients might avoid trading with you, because Sole Traders are often seen as 'small fry', with too much vested in one person. (Obviously this depends on the sector and your USP.)

PARTNERSHIP

If you are planning on setting up your business with a partner or partners, then a formal Partnership operates rather like a Sole Trader.

- **PROS OF PARTNERSHIP:** Quicker and easier to set up than a limited company. It's the expected norm in some industries, notably accountants, lawyers etc.

A BUSINESS PARTNERSHIP *can be successful if there is ongoing mutual trust, good communication and a healthy spirit of cooperation between the partners. Going into partnership with friends or relations will test those relationships to the limit. It's not suited to everyone!*

- **CONS OF PARTNERSHIP:** You really have to trust your partners. Each partner is 'jointly and severally liable' for the debts of the partnership. That means if you take out a business loan together but your partner declares bankruptcy… you then owe the lot!

Partners are liable for all debts and obligations of the business, and in a normal partnership that can be unlimited. However, it is possible to set up a Limited Liability Partnership (LLP), where each partner contributes a certain amount of money to the Partnership and is not liable for anything over that amount.

If you are considering setting up a Partnership then you should draw up a Deed of Partnership with the help of a solicitor.

LIMITED COMPANY

There are three main types of Limited Company: a private company limited by shares; a private company limited by guarantee, which is usually a non-profit organization with guarantors rather than shareholders; and a public limited company (plc), whose shares can be traded on the Stock Exchange.

As a first-time entrepreneur, you are most likely to set up a private company limited by shares. This means you will become a director and shareholder in the company.

A private company limited by shares, commonly referred to as a 'Limited Company' or just 'Ltd', raises its money by selling shares. Shares can be bought by you and other directors as well as any other people you may choose to work with or accept investment from. The shareholders' liability is limited to any amount remaining unpaid on

THE TANGLE TEEZER *was invented by Shaun Pulfrey. At the time when Shaun visited the Den in Series 5 he was operating as a Sole Trader with his fledgling enterprise based on this revolutionary type of hairbrush. He didn't get any investment from the Dragons, but soon after set up as a Limited Company, taking out a director's loan to cover the business's start-up costs. See how he fared on pp120–1.*

the shares they own (typically zero). The company is considered to be a legal entity in its own right and its directors must work in the best interests of the company. Profit made by the company stays within the company until it is paid out in the form of salary to employees or dividends to shareholders. Directors of the company can be both employees and shareholders. Company profits are subject to corporation tax, which is higher than basic-rate income tax but lower than higher-rate income tax.

A typical scenario for a small business might be: two directors, each of whom owns half the shares and does half the work. Each director draws a small salary (just below their tax-free allowance), and then tops up their income in the form of dividends. This may save them tax compared with working as a Partnership and paying income tax on their profits.

- **PROS OF LIMITED COMPANY:** Your small business may appear more legitimate if it is a Limited Company rather than a Sole Trader or Partnership, while at the same time limiting your personal liability to any losses incurred by your business and reducing the tax you have to pay. If you have a very small business, you can even set up a one-person Limited Company.

- **CONS OF LIMITED COMPANY:** By law you have to register with Companies House and fulfil various obligations (see pages 70–73). You need to employ the services of a qualified accountant. Some finance organizations recognize that more directors of small Limited Companies go bankrupt than any other job title, so it can be difficult getting a mortgage! Moreover, a business loan raised against a personal asset such as your house will not be protected by the company's limited liability status.

MAX MCMURDO *(see pp88–9) says that, since making the transition from a Sole Trader to a Limited Company, he has become far more of a businessman: "I look at the world in a different way. I constantly analyse shops and products and even design with price points in mind, which was something that I never really considered before."*

Choosing a suitable structure for your start-up is an important decision. If you are unsure, then it would be a good idea to speak to an accountant, your bank manager, your local Business Link or local Chamber of Commerce. They can also help you to set up in business by advising on record keeping, software, training, networking events and marketing opportunities.

PREPARE FOR TAXATION

The Revenue and Customs produces, and updates annually, a good basic guide to all matters to do with setting up a business in relation to tax and national insurance. It is in a pdf format and can be downloaded from the 'Starting Up' section of www.hmrc.gov.uk.

TAXATION FOR SOLE TRADERS AND PARTNERSHIPS

When you become self-employed as a sole trader or a partner you must register for income tax and national insurance (NI) purposes with HM Revenue and Customs (HMRC). You must register as soon as you start working for yourself; you cannot register in advance but if you delay registering, you may have to pay a penalty. You need to provide quite a bit of basic information so don't expect it to be a two-minute task, though if you are registering as a Sole Trader or a Partner in a normal Partnership you can register online via the HMRC website, or by telephone.

If you are setting up a Partnership, each Partner must register separately. If you're setting up an LLP you can only register by post. There is up-to-date information on Partnerships and setting them up at www.hmrc.gov.uk/partnerships. You can download the appropriate forms from this site as well.

TAXATION FOR CONTRACTORS IN THE CONSTRUCTION INDUSTRY

If your business – whether Sole Trader, Partnership or Limited Company – will be operating as a contractor and/or a sub-contractor in the construction industry, you must also register with the Construction Industry Scheme – see www.hmrc.gov.uk/cis for more information.

OBLIGATIONS AND TAXATION FOR LIMITED COMPANIES

The red tape and taxation is more complex for a Limited Company than for Sole Trader or Partnership, and you will need to make contact with **COMPANIES HOUSE** (www.companieshouse.gov.uk).

- **COMPANY REGISTRATION.** Your company must be registered at Companies House. You will be sent a Certificate of Incorporation if accepted.

- **MEMORANDA AND ARTICLES OF ASSOCIATION.** There are template kits available for these legal documents, but you might want to consult a solicitor if you are unsure how the wording relates to your proposed business.

- **REGISTERED OFFICE.** You must have a registered office. This could be your main place of work or perhaps your accountant's office.

- **COMPANY DIRECTORS.** A Limited Company must have at least one Director.

- **UNIQUE COMPANY NAME.** Your company name mustn't replicate any other existing company. You can check for names on the Companies House website.

- **ANNUAL ACCOUNTS.** The annual accounts must be filed at Companies House. Your accountant will help you create and submit these.

- **ANNUAL RETURN.** An annual return must be submitted each year, updating Companies House with the basic details of the company.

- **ANNUAL CORPORATION TAX RETURN.** A corporation tax return must be submitted each year and due taxes paid within nine months of the company financial year-end.

- **DECLARATION FOR TAX PURPOSES.** The Revenue and Customs must be informed if the company has any profits or taxable income in a financial year.

- **EMPLOYEES' PAYE AND NATIONAL INSURANCE.** Anyone employed by the company – directors, full-time employees, part-time employees and casual staff – must pay income tax and national insurance on their income.

- **EMPLOYER'S NATIONAL INSURANCE.** These payments are different from employees' national insurance, and paid on top of gross salary.

KNOW A DIRECTOR'S OFFICIAL RESPONSIBILITIES

Presuming that you are going to be a director of the company it is worth looking at the personal obligations you take on in that role.

You can and should employ the services of an accountant to prepare the accounts, but ultimately *you are personally responsible* for ensuring that the following financial and other tasks are carried out:

- **MAINTAINING FINANCIAL RECORDS**, from which company accounts can be prepared, that give a 'true and fair representation' of the financial situation of the company.

- **SUBMITTING THE COMPANY ACCOUNTS**, on time, to Companies House.

- **SUBMITTING THE ANNUAL RETURN TO COMPANIES HOUSE.** (This is different to your tax returns.)

- **SUBMITTING THE CORPORATION TAX RETURN TO HMRC** and paying any corporation tax due.

- **ENSURING THE CORRECT PAYMENT OF STAFF**, including yourself and any other directors, plus taking responsibility for the deduction of income tax and national insurance contributions, where appropriate.

- **TRADING IN A SOLVENT POSITION**; this means that you must ensure at all times that you are able to meet the financial liabilities of your business.

- **NOTIFYING COMPANIES HOUSE IF YOU CHANGE YOUR REGISTERED COMPANY ADDRESS.**

- **INFORMING COMPANIES HOUSE OF ANY CHANGES IN THE PARTICULARS OF COMPANY DIRECTOR(S) OR SECRETARY.** For instance if you and your spouse are directors and you separate, you must inform Companies House.

- **ALWAYS ACTING IN THE INTERESTS OF THE COMPANY SHAREHOLDERS.** This means that the directors cannot enrich themselves in a way that damages the company. So if you and your spouse are directors and shareholders and you separate you must beware taking cash out of the business without your spouse's consent!

Chapter 5 covers more detail of actually managing the finances.

UNDERSTAND VALUE ADDED TAX (VAT)

Whether you are operating as a Sole Trader, Partnership or Limited Company, if your turnover reaches a certain level in any 12-month period, you're legally required to charge VAT for your goods or

"THE HARDEST THING IN THE WORLD TO UNDERSTAND IS THE INCOME TAX " ALBERT EINSTEIN

services. The threshold for mandatory VAT registration at the time of writing (in the spring of 2010) is £68,000, and the rate is 17.5%. Note that the threshold refers to *turnover* – the total annual net sales of your business – not profit.

You must pass the VAT you've charged on to HMRC every quarter. At the same time, you are entitled to claim back the VAT you have paid for certain goods and services and deduct that from what you owe. In effect this appears to reduce the gross price you pay for certain business expenses.

You can register voluntarily for VAT even if your turnover is less than the threshold. This makes sense if your business purchases a lot of materials. On the other hand, the addition of VAT can be a major issue if your target customers are private individuals who cannot themselves claim back VAT, and your competitors are operating below the VAT threshold – your product or service will be more expensive by default.

HOW TO CALCULATE VAT

NB The net price is without VAT; the gross price includes VAT. The formulas show VAT calculations at 17.5%, which is the rate at the time of writing but likely to increase at short notice.

If you know the net price (e.g. what you want to charge for your product or service before adding VAT), this is the formula you need to use to calculate the VAT:

Net price x 0.175 = VAT

e.g. if your net price is £10
£10 x 0.175 = £1.75

Thus your gross price is
£10 + £1.75 = £11.75

Sometimes you might want to jump straight from the net price to gross price, in which case you can use this formula:

Net price x 1.175 = gross price

e.g. if your net price is £10
£10 x 1.175 = £11.75

The VAT portion is the difference between gross and net figures, in this case £1.75

If, by contrast, you know the gross price (e.g. you've bought something for your business in a shop) and want to calculate the net price and VAT from it for your VAT return, this is the formula:

Gross price ÷ 1.175 = net price

e.g. if your gross price is £10
£10 ÷ 1.175 = £8.51

The VAT portion is the difference between gross and net figures, in this case £1.49

HOW THE CHARGING AND RECLAIMING OF VAT WORKS

Let's say you buy a necessary tool for your business with a net cost of £10. The business you buy from is VAT registered so adds 17.5% VAT (£1.75) to the net cost. The gross price you pay for the tool is £11.75.

In the meantime, you do a job for a customer and charge them £100. You are VAT registered so you add 17.5% VAT (£17.50) to the net cost. The customer pays you £117.50.

At the end of the quarter you fill in your VAT return and pay the HMRC the VAT received minus the VAT paid, in this case £17.50 minus £1.75, which comes to £15.75.

You should be able to see from this that it might be beneficial for you to register for VAT, even if your turnover is under the threshold. You will soon get used to using these simple formulas when calculating VAT and submitting your VAT return. However, the downside is that the rules about what VAT applies to can be complicated, as you will see below. There are also frequent changes to the rules as well as different rules for goods and services bought from inside or outside the EU.

VAT-EXEMPT GOODS AND SERVICES

Although most goods and services are subject to VAT, some things are exempt, notably the following:

- Insurance, finance and credit
- Education and training by schools and colleges (but other forms of training are subject to VAT at the full rate)
- Fund-raising events by charities
- Postal services provided by Royal Mail
- Subscriptions to membership organizations
- Selling, leasing and letting of commercial land and buildings (though exemption can be waived)
- Physical education and sports activities

MAILING COSTS *through Royal Mail are exempt from VAT, whereas courier services are subject to VAT at the full rate.*

If you sell only VAT-exempt goods or services, you cannot register for VAT, which means you can't reclaim any VAT on your purchases.

ZERO-RATED GOODS AND SERVICES

Some goods and services are subject to VAT, but the rate is zero, which obviously creates confusion with VAT-exempt items. These are some (by no means all) of the things that are zero-rated:

- Food (but not alcohol, confectionery, soft drinks or food used in catering)
- Books, magazines, newspapers (but currently not e-books)
- Printed or copied music (but currently not music CDs)
- Children's clothing
- Public transport
- Equipment for disabled people
- Construction and sale of new domestic buildings

THE E-BOOK AND THE PRINTED BOOK: *the former is currently subject to the standard rate of VAT whereas the latter is zero-rated.*

REDUCED-RATED GOODS AND SERVICES

Currently, the rate on reduced-rated goods and services is 5%. These are some of the things that are reduced-rated:

ALTHOUGH CHILDRENS' CAR SEATS HAVE A REDUCED-RATE OF VAT *applied to their sales, push chairs and items such as the Buggyboot (right; see also p187) are not treated similarly.*

- Electricity and gas for domestic and residential use (but fuel for business use is standard-rated)
- Renovating an empty residential building
- Children's car seats

From all this, you will appreciate that you need to check the VAT status of your product or service from the outset, and that you must take care when completing a VAT return that you do not try to reclaim VAT on zero-rated, reduced-rated or exempt items. VAT inspectors have a right to check your records at any time without any real notice, and if they disagree with your figures they are relentless. Fines and prosecutions are part of their arsenal.

If you do become VAT registered you must keep your accounts up-to-date and you must by law submit your VAT return and any payment due within a month of each financial quarter.

Once you are trading and getting close to the threshold, consider registering early so you don't have to try to collect VAT for payments you've already received.

If your business turns over between £68,000 and £150,000 per year (2010 thresholds), you can negotiate a flat-rate percentage of turnover to pay the VAT… but you have to agree this in advance with the HMRC and they will want to see evidence that the percentage is appropriate.

KNOW AN EMPLOYER'S OBLIGATIONS TO STAFF

If you're planning to take on staff, you need to bear in mind that employers have the following obligations to employees:

- **PAYMENT.** To pay the employee the agreed amount if the employee arrives for work and is able to work.

- **PROVIDING THE EMPLOYEE WITH WORK TO DO.** This is limited, however, for example, if the employee is paid on commission the employer must simply provide the employee with the capacity to work.

- **OBSERVING HEALTH & SAFETY REGULATIONS.** In principle this means that an employer must provide:
  - **SAFE SYSTEMS OF WORK**
  - **A SAFE PLACE OF WORK**
  - **PLANT, MACHINERY AND EQUIPMENT THAT IS SAFE TO USE**
  - **COMPETENT SUPERVISION AND/OR SUITABLE TRAINING**
  - **CARE IN THE SELECTION OF FELLOW EMPLOYEES**

  (See www.hse.gov.uk for more information about health and safety requirements.)

- **STATEMENT OF RIGHTS.** Give employees correct information about their rights in their contract of employment.

- **OFFICIAL CHANNEL FOR COMPLAINTS.** Give employees reasonable opportunity to have their complaints looked at.

- **DUTY OF MUTUAL TRUST & CONFIDENCE.** The employer and employee must show respect for each other. Examples of breaches of 'mutual trust' would be:
  - **HARASSING, BULLYING OR VICTIMIZING OF AN EMPLOYEE.** Note that this is almost certain to also be a breach of any one of many Employment Acts such as the Human Rights Act, the Disability Discrimination Act or the Employment Equality Act.
  - **PHYSICAL VIOLENCE BY EMPLOYER OR EMPLOYEE.**
  - **THEFT BY EMPLOYEE.**

- **HOLIDAY ENTITLEMENT, SICK PAY ETC.** An employee is entitled to at least four weeks' holiday per year, along with Statutory Sick Pay and Statutory Maternity Pay.

WITH A BUSINESS SUCH AS UK COMMERCIAL CLEANING *(see also pp35, 219), in which dealing with toxic substances is part and parcel of their work, adequate protective clothing for the workforce is one of the most important concerns. As a company, they must keep abreast of any changes to health and safety legislation.*

EMPLOYERS' LIABILITY INSURANCE

Under the terms of the Employers' Liability (Compulsory Insurance) Act (1969), if you employ people and if any of your employees are normally based in England, Scotland or Wales (including offshore installations or associated structures) you must have Employers' Liability Insurance. Your business is only exempt if it is purely a family business, i.e. if all of your employees are closely related to you. However, this exemption does not apply to family businesses which are incorporated as Limited Companies.

The Employers' Liability Insurance must be provided by an authorized insurer (see www.fsa.gov.uk for a list of acceptable organizations). You must display a copy of the certificate of insurance where your employees can easily read it. You are allowed to display your certificate electronically but if you choose this method you need to ensure your employees know how and where to find the certificate and that you provide them reasonable access to it. The Health and Safety Executive website (www.hse.gov.uk) has more details.

COMMON MISUNDERSTANDINGS ABOUT EMPLOYERS' OBLIGATIONS

There is an obligation on an employer to pay Statutory Sick Pay for the first 28 weeks an employee is absent due to sickness in any period of three years, if the employee is eligible, but there is no legal duty to pay Contractual Sick Pay.

New employers often do not realize that part of Statutory Sick Pay and up to 100% of Statutory Maternity Pay is recoverable through employer's national insurance, so long as certain criteria are fulfilled. See the HMRC website (www.hmrc.gov.uk) for more details.

An employer has no legal duty to provide references to an employee or ex-employee (except where the reference is required by the Financial Service Authority). However, if a reference is provided there is a duty to make sure the reference is completed with 'reasonable skill and care' and is 'true, accurate and fair'. This duty to the employee extends to a duty to the addressee of the reference not to make any 'negligent' statements about the employee.

KNOW YOUR OBLIGATIONS TO CUSTOMERS

There is a plethora of law and trading standards in this country (both UK law and EU law). There is also different law relating to consumers as opposed to business customers. Over the page is a brief summing up of the primary matters.

" AN OUNCE OF PREVENTION IS WORTH A POUND OF CURE "

OLD ENGLISH ADAGE

SALE OF GOODS ACT 1979

This Act states that goods (i.e. tangible things rather than services) must fit the description used in any advert, label or packaging etc that relates to them – such as the year or make, type, colour, size or materials used. The goods must also be of satisfactory quality and should be fit for their purpose.

CONSUMER PROTECTION ACT 1987

This says that only safe goods should be put on sale. It also expressly prohibits misleading price indications.

SUPPLY OF GOODS AND SERVICES ACT 1982

This states that work covered by the contract (and a contract is deemed to exist as soon as you agree to a request to carry out work for someone) must be carried out with reasonable skill and care, within a reasonable time, and for a reasonable price (if no price has actually been agreed). The difficult bit of this legislation is that 'reasonable' is not defined by law. If something goes wrong as a result of your work the customer can ask you to put the work right, and if you won't, they are legally entitled to employ another contractor to rectify the problem and claim the costs from you.

UNFAIR CONTRACT TERMS ACT 1977 AND UNFAIR TERMS IN CONSUMER CONTRACTS REGULATIONS 1999

If terms in pre-printed contracts (the 'small print', to coin a phrase) are unreasonable, the Office of Fair Trading can make you change the contract. These regulations apply only to standard contracts and not to a specifically negotiated agreement.

IF CONTRACTS *are going to feature in your line of business, hire a solicitor to draft up or check the wording to ensure you are complying with the law and also that your own interests are protected.*

CONSUMER CREDIT ACT 1974

If your customer buys your goods or services (for over £100) with a credit card, their credit card company is also liable for the faulty goods or services. If they buy on hire purchase or other credit arranged by you and you will not put things right they can claim from the finance company.

If in any doubt contact your local Trading Standards Officer (www.tradingstandards.gov.uk).

CHECK IF YOU NEED PROFESSIONAL INDEMNITY INSURANCE

Many businesses carry Professional Indemnity Insurance. This insurance protects a professional or business against legal liability towards third parties for injury, loss, or damage arising from his or her own professional negligence or that of the business's employees. In some sectors this is a pre-requisite of being considered as a supplier

PHOTOGRAPHERS *are among those who often need Public Liability Insurance along with Employers' Liability Insurance, Contents Insurance and adequate Health & Safety precautions – their lighting equipment has been known to trip up people and cause fires.*

and for some professions it is a requirement of the institute or body. For example the Law Society insists that all solicitors' firms must take out insurance to the value of £1,000,000 or more to cover defective work or fraud by that firm.

If you belong to a trade or professional association this insurance is often discounted. Professional Indemnity Insurance may seem expensive when you first get a quote, but it is usually good value in comparison with having to re-do a job or pay compensation.

Professional Indemnity premiums vary enormously depending on what you declare as the 'nature of business'. For example, if you are a 'training consultant' the premiums are often 20% lower than a 'management consultant', though the work may be very similar.

KNOW YOUR OBLIGATIONS TO THE PUBLIC AT LARGE

You must ensure that your business doesn't present a hazard to the public. This means that you have to ensure that your personnel, premises and vehicles, tools and equipment are safe and comply with all relevant regulations.

Whilst not directly a Health and Safety issue, it is also important that your premises are legally operating for the purpose you use them for. If you simply use a computer in your dining room to run your business and you receive no visitors then you can operate from home with no problems, but if you convert your double garage into a pottery and run day-long pottery classes there twice a month, you need to get a Change of Use Consent from the Local Authority, or a Certificate of Lawful Development (it depends on the Local Authority in your area). If you do not obtain this, or you make material changes to the property and fail to get Building Regulations Approval, you may find that your insurance is invalidated.

Your obligations to the public are an area where you can insure against loss, through Public Liability Insurance. This covers any awards of damages given to a member of the public because of an injury or damage to their property caused by you or your business. It also covers any related legal fees, costs and expenses as well as costs of hospital treatment (including ambulance costs) that the NHS may claim from you. If you run any premises where the public visit, you are very strongly advised to carry Public Liability Insurance, and again it is often a pre-requisite of some customers.

REESTORE

Max McMurdo started up Reestore in 2002 whilst designing cars in Germany. Reestore was, in effect, an identity for environmental furniture products, made using recycled materials. Examples included a chair made from an old shopping trolley, a chair from a wheelbarrow and Ben the Bin, two small sheets of recycled plastic that transformed an old plastic carrier bag into a bin by lending a rigid structure.

MAX IN THE DEN *with Ben the Bin.*

Several councils had expressed an interest in the bin – to send out to residents in flats – and high profile individuals and high-end design shops had bought items of furniture. However, nothing was thus far profitable in a meaningful way, and Max had been subsidizing his income from Reestore by taking on part-time work.

Once he had secured investment in the Den from Deborah and Theo during Series 5, Max had to negotiate the change from being a Sole Trader to a small business. The upside of this was that Max could work full-time on the design, manufacture and sale of his furniture; the downside was that he had to get to grips with the commercial side of business. He had to learn about distribution, outsourcing and ultimately trusting others with his ideas and vision. "I found it very hard to let go and employ other manufacturers to take on some of the production. This is not uncommon for creative types, as we tend to be overly passionate about our work."

Max eventually let a distributer handle the mass-produced items, such as Ben the Bin. An office manager was employed for logistics, and local fabricators were used for much of the manufacturing. Max now sees the bespoke pieces as his "babies – where I can get my creative kicks" – while the mass-produced items generate royalties and offer a more commercial, less emotional process. "Letting go and compromising have been the key in turning a one-man band into an eco design business."

ONE OF MAX'S EARLY DESIGNS *was a shopping trolley chair (top). He has also made a chaise longue from a roll-top bath and an internally lit coffee table from the drum of a washing machine.*

COMMANDMENT 4

PLAN TO SUCCEED

Want to write a brilliant business plan?

ON DRAGONS' DEN most of the questions that the Dragons, as potential investors and business partners, put to the contestants relate to their business plan. "Who is going to buy this?" "How much do you need to take this to market and how did you come by that figure?" "What is the sale price and how much margin does that create?" You can answer all such questions with confidence when you write a business plan. And the exercise is not just for those rarefied Dragon appearances. All businesses, large and small, should begin life with a well-constructed business plan. This chapter explains what you need to cover in your business plan – and why.

Are excuses flooding your mind, putting you off writing a business plan? Is it because no one is going to pay you to make a plan, whereas if you get out there and start trading you will get paid straight away? Are you a specialist in your trade or profession, and feel that planning and writing documents isn't really your thing? Or do you reckon the plan is so clear in your mind that you don't need to write it down? Or do you believe that because plans always have to be changed, it's pointless making a formal plan at all (let's face it, how do you know how much you are going to sell?).

There are probably other excuses, but you get the point!

GOOD REASONS TO WRITE A BUSINESS PLAN

Many small businesses start without a formal business plan, but here are four good reasons to write one:

1 The creation of a sensible and meaningful business plan forces you to think through the matters in a coherent way. Arguably this is the most important reason.

2 You will definitely need to show a business plan if you want to raise funds of any sort.

3 The business plan will impress prospective staff, business partners, suppliers and customers.

4 The plan will remind you of what you are trying to achieve when either you are struggling or so busy that you lose sight of your original motivation.

> **" REDUCE YOUR PLAN TO WRITING. THE MOMENT YOU COMPLETE THIS, YOU WILL HAVE DEFINITELY GIVEN CONCRETE FORM TO THE INTANGIBLE DESIRE. "** NAPOLEON HILL
(1883–1970), AUTHOR OF 'THINK AND GROW RICH'

WHAT IS THE FOCUS OF THE PLAN?

First thing to decide is what the main purpose of the business plan is. Who will be its primary audience?

For instance, the bank manager will want to see a business plan when considering you for a business loan, but the bank manager will also probably demand collateral security for the loan – your house for example. Consequently the bank manager has security for the loan regardless of the success of the business.

By contrast, a business investor is risking his or her money on the success of the business; the investor only gets a return relating to the profits of the business. So the investor will need to be convinced that the business idea is sound, that the market is there and that you are credible.

Meanwhile, a Dragon-like business partner – someone who is going to invest both money and expertise – will want to assess not only your credibility to the market but also whether they can work with you.

WHAT A BUSINESS PLAN NEEDS TO COVER

There is no universally accepted format for a business plan. Pretty much every bank offers their suggested template – the Business Link offers theirs at www.businesslink.gov.uk, and there are dozens of online advisors offering versions. They do all contain the material listed in the bullet points below, though, so make sure you cover these basic categories, whatever format you use. The finished document should begin with an executive summary, then go into more detail on topics that seem necessary for both the audience of your plan and your own personal or business use.

- **EXECUTIVE SUMMARY**
- **A DESCRIPTION OF YOUR BUSINESS IDEA**, whether it is a product or a service
- **THE OBJECTIVES AND STRATEGIES OF THE BUSINESS**
- **AN ANALYSIS OF THE MARKET**
- **THE MONEY MATTERS** – everything from capital to cash flow, sales and cost projections and finance requirements
- **THE PEOPLE** – even if this is a one-person enterprise

THE EXECUTIVE SUMMARY

The initial summary is often the single most important part of your plan if you are seeking funding or support from others. It is a little like the introduction for a presentation to the Dragons. If you don't convince people in the couple of minutes it takes to read the summary then they won't bother to go any further. Don't try to write the summary first… rather you should tackle writing it only after

Summary of Business Plan for "Met-alex" Metalwork

Proposed Trading Style
Sole trader; aiming to work within a 30-mile radius of base.

Activities
Design, making and installation of architectural metalwork, including gates, banisters, lintels, weather vanes, signs, armillaries, sundials and hand-forged knife blades. Also auto welding and repair of farm machinery.

Customers
Residential dwellings, office buildings, farms, churches, engineering firms, architects and small builders firms, garden centres, craft shops. On-line sales.

USP
Bespoke metalwork, to your design, on your doorstep from a local craftsman… see him in action.

Communication
- Already have contacts at some garages, small builders and fencing contractors.
- Leaflet drop to farms, car body shops and other contractors.
- Card drop to local residences, pubs and parish councils.
- Sale or return sculptures at local garden centres and craft shops; leaflets available beside sculptures.
- Larger sculpture donated to local "sponsor a roundabout" scheme (with signs).
- Magnetic signs on sides of van.
- Logos on overalls and sweatshirts.
- "A" boards to put up when working on site.
- Small ad in local life magazine.
- Link ad on regional "best-of" website.
- PR to get a puff in local paper.
- Website with a small online shop selling items mail order and taking small commissions if possible.
- eBay sales of sculptures and small manufactured items.

Got already: van, arc weld

Startup Funding Need

Generator, oxy acetyle
Business cards, leafle
Sponsor a roundab

Business is sup
metalwork co
investing in

Principal a
and store

Sales
Reta
Co
Repair w

Year One	Retail	Commission	400	
Quarter	1000	600	500	3500
One	1400	800	700	4200
Two	1800	1000	900	
Three	2100	1200		
Four		**Year One total sales £12,400**		

Year Two	Retail	Commission	Repair	Quarter total
Quarter		1400	900	4900
One	2600	1600	900	5500
Two	3000	2000	900	6300
Three	3400	2200	900	7300
Four	4200	**Year Two total sales £24,000**		

MANY DRAGONS' DEN ENTREPRENEURS *make bold claims for their businesses in terms of future profits, but it's also true that many go on to exceed their forecasts. One such was Paul Ward (right) of Paragon PE, a company selling antimicrobial cleaning products. In Series 7, Paul outlined strong trading figures, edging up from £250,000 profit in the first year to £500,000 in the following year and £750,000 profit in year three. Within a few months of the programme airing, his company surpassed its year one figures and the business has since been valued at more than £4 million.*

you've written up the rest of the full plan, then insert the summary at the front of the document. You don't literally have to call it 'executive summary', but you should summarize these points:

- **PURPOSE OF THE PLAN** – to raise money, set out plan for partners etc
- **NATURE OF THE PRODUCT OR SERVICE**
- **USP**
- **POTENTIAL MARKET**
- **REALISTIC FORECASTS OF INCOME AND COSTS**
- **CREDIBILITY OF PEOPLE INVOLVED**
- **FINANCE REQUIREMENTS** – how much you need and what you need it for
- **LEGAL STRUCTURE** – is it Sole Trader, a Partnership, a Limited Company, or something else? This matters to others because it has implications for recovering losses if your business fails.

" PEOPLE WITHOUT THE ACADEMICS THINK THAT THEY CAN COME UP WITH AN IDEA IN THE MORNING AND IT'S GOING TO CHANGE THEIR LIVES. THEY DON'T UNDERSTAND THAT IT'S NOT JUST ABOUT THE IDEA. IT'S THE EXECUTION – HAVING A PLAN, A STRATEGY, UNDERSTANDING YOUR MARKET AND THE COMMERCIAL FINANCIAL DYNAMICS, WHERE YOU BUY PRODUCTS FROM, HOW YOU PRICE AND SELL THEM. " JAMES CAAN, DRAGON

In all, your executive summary should be only one or two pages in length; any longer and it isn't a summary!

THE BUSINESS IDEA

After the summary, you should set out the big picture. Give an overview of your industry or market sector, both current and projected, explaining the business opportunity and why it will succeed. Describe your offering in a non-technical way, focusing on what you will do to make your business stand out.

If you are seeking support for research and development with your start-up, explain what you have done so far and why you believe that you can develop a winning product or service.

If you find it difficult to produce this section clearly and simply, then you probably have not thought it through properly. Stop writing and go back to thinking!

BLINDS IN A BOX

In their pitch to the Dragons, Dominic Lawrence, Simeone Salik and Janice Dalton demonstrated a clear business plan for selling their product (instant paper blinds).

JANICE DALTON, DOMINIC LAWRENCE AND SIMEONE SALIK, WITH INVESTMENT PARTNER JAMES CAAN, *finding a new use for their paper blinds.*

They had looked at how a similar product was selling in the USA and identified potential markets for the product in the UK: wholesale to DIY stores and to individual customers using a dedicated website. They were also positioned to tender for the athletes' village at the 2012 Olympic Games in London. All this gave them solid enough reasons to push the business plan forward.

They next looked at manufacturing, and found a low-cost producer of the blinds in the Far East, which kept their production costs as low as possible. Their weakest point was that, because they had not invented the paper blind, they were not in a position to patent it. However, they had addressed this issue too. They had contacted the inventor in the

USA, and he had agreed to let them sell the blinds in the UK without infringing his patent.

Nevertheless, without the security of a patent, they recognized the need to move fast and secure market share before imitators encroached on their business. So, while they had already begun selling decent numbers of the blinds on the internet, they also realized that they would need capital investment and good commercial connections to increase the impetus.

The investment and bringing Dragons on board was thus a strategic ploy to raise the profile of their product and to gain a foothold in the distribution to the wholesale market. They knew they would have to give away a large chunk of the business, but they calculated that this was worthwhile in terms of the business benefits.

THE PAPER BLINDS *are geared towards temporary use. They provide instant privacy and security when moving into a new home, for example. A secondary market is for student accommodation and other short-term occupancies.*

OBJECTIVES AND STRATEGIES

Set out your objectives and explain how are you going to achieve them. For each objective, define your strategy, and for each strategy, describe your tactics – how and when you will implement the steps to reach it. Here's an example:

OBJECTIVE
Turnover of £55,000 in year one

STRATEGY
To gain six new corporate customers buying a total of 10 training workshops in the second, third and fourth quarters

TACTICS

❶ Advertise free taster sessions to 30 organizations identified as segment targets

❷ Run four tasters in Q1 each with at least five organizations' buyers represented

❸ Convert at least two in five of these buyers into paying clients, offering a money back guarantee if not delighted with service

❹ Run first two paid-for workshops in Q2, four in Q3 and four in Q4

Make sure your objectives are **SMART**: Specific, Measurable, Achievable, Realistic and Time-bound. For instance: "To become a top ten supplier by market share within the next four years." "To gross £100,000 turnover and £25,000 pre-tax profit by 2013." "To achieve a positive return on investment by the end of this financial year."

THE MARKET

Pull all of the raw data from your market research into a clear description of the current market, your target audience and your competition. Make sure that you cover the points that follow.

VICTORIA MCGRANE OF FASHION LABEL NEUROTICA *had been working in the high-end niche market, selling to exclusive boutiques, and could see more profitability in the high street chain store fashion sector. To target this market, she felt that a distinct new label was needed. Find out how things have progressed for Victoria on pp140–1.*

THE MARKET – SIZE

How many potential buyers are there for your business? If you're proposing a local service, then just look at potential customers in your geographic area. If you're proposing a national service, then break down the market into areas where your business will fly.

CLIVE BILLING'S CASE *was not dissimilar to Victoria's (see previous page). He had traded in expensive diamond jewellery for years, and he too recognized that there was more profit to be made in the lower sector of the market, where the jewellery was cheaper and sales swifter. He already had a website for his existing business and, rather than adapt that, he felt he needed to tailor a new site to the market sector he was now targeting.*

CLIVE NOW HAS TWO DISTINCT SITES: *one (above) for high-end sales and another (right) for the cheaper sector. While both run profitably, the one for the cheaper sector is on target to soon outstrip its sister operation.*

THE MARKET – CONDITION

Is the market stable, growing or declining? Explain any changes you see in the market and what effect you anticipate this having on your business. Include market history if it is relevant. Then again, there may not be any if your product or service is truly innovative!

THE MARKET – SEGMENTS

Analyse market segments by pricing, quality or any other clear criterion. You'll have a better chance of success if you focus on specific segments. Determining the right target audience is probably the most important part of your marketing efforts – it doesn't matter what you're selling if you're not trying to sell it to the right people!

Go into as much detail as possible. Describe your typical customer. For a business-to-consumer (B2C) market, define the age group, gender, family size and income. For business-to-business (B2B), make sure you include industry type, company size, job titles/departments of buyers. Include such influences as spending patterns, brand consciousness, buying behaviour and what promotional or marketing efforts seem to work.

YOUR STRENGTHS AND OPPORTUNITIES

Here you define and explain your business's USP and all the other strengths that you will exploit to achieve your objectives. These might be the expertise of the people, the innovative nature of the product or service, the gap in the market, or the weakness of the current provision or even a specific competitor.

IN HIS PITCH FOR A TELEPHONE SCREENING DEVICE CALLED TRUECALL, *Steve Smith elucidated the threats to his business from competition. This came in the form of products offered by telephone companies to provide anonymous caller rejection and caller blocking services. He explained that customers would pay about £50 a year for such services typically through monthly tariffs, and argued that his device, which had more functionality and a one-off payment of about £100, could be proven to be better value to the customer.*

YOUR WEAKNESSES AND THREATS TO YOUR BUSINESS

A weakness identified is a weakness half cured. Similarly, a threat recognized is a threat that is countered, which is why it is critical to consider these areas. This may be as simple as not having enough experienced sales staff, or having no market presence as a newcomer. Note all possible threats to your business such as aggressive competition, government regulation and environmental concerns. Give a complete and thorough overview of the competitive market.

THE 'MARKETING MIX'

The 'Marketing Mix' is made up of the four 'P's of Position, Price, Promotion and Place. Commandment 6 looks at the Marketing Mix in more detail, but here is a summary for your business plan:

- **POSITION.** State how you will position your product or service. For example will it be a premium brand (exclusive, expensive and aspirational) or an economy brand (cheap, cheerful and accessible)?

- **PRICE.** State how you are pricing your offering. This follows on from position but also in direct relationship to the competitors' pricing and the market capacity.

- **PROMOTION.** State how you are going to promote your product/service amongst your target market. This may stretch from almost any medium for advertising, through trade shows, door knocking, direct sales or third party agents. You need to plan according to the objective of each promotional act. For example, are you trying to build brand-awareness, generate interest, encourage enquiries or make immediate sales?

- **PLACE.** State how you are going to distribute your product or service. In the case of a tangible product, this might be through retail chains, online sales, agents or direct sales. Compare this with the standard distribution channels for your industry, and explain the strengths and weaknesses of your chosen methods. In the case of a service offering, you might be describing how you would deal with and exploit opportunities outside your geographic area if that is relevant. This could be through a joint venture or a partner organization.

SALES FORECASTS

Sales forecasting is not an exact science, but you have to exercise judgement based on a combination of your market research and your financial needs. The former gives you clues as to what you can expect; the latter is a motivating driver of what you need to be aiming for. From

IT ALL LOOKS POSITIVE AND PRETTY – *but make sure you base your sales forecasts on real market research and a calculation of what you must sell in order to keep trading.*

this you can calculate specific targets for periods (which may become milestones marking progress towards achieving your business goals) or salespeople (which form the basis of their performance management and hence, reward).

THE MONEY MATTERS

The primary function of a business, even a 'lifestyle business', is to make money, so the financial aspects of a business plan are critical. The type of funding you require will dictate how your plan is written. Investors will want to know how and when they are going to see profit, whilst lenders will want to see how you will repay the loan.

At the heart of the money section of your business plan are the **PROFIT & LOSS STATEMENT** and **CASH FLOW STATEMENT**. These will

THE SPIT 'N' POLISH SHOESHINE COMPANY *(above left; see also pp134–5)* and **KCO ICEBLADING** *(above right, see also pp58–9) are two contrasting businesses that both offered more than one revenue stream. For Spit 'n' Polish, revenue would come not only from shoe shining but also from advertising on the in-booth screen. For the Iceblading business, revenue would be generated through the sale of skates and through tuition in skating classes. Multiple revenue streams can be a great way to increase your revenue, but they can also cause distractions from the core business. Their worth needs to be carefully scrutinized.*

all be projections for a start-up. Break down your projections into monthly periods for the first two years and then move to annual periods. See below for more detail about these vital documents.

If you are seeking funds it is only reasonable that those investing or lending know precisely what you are intending to do with the money. So provide a breakdown of **CAPITAL NEEDS**, to cover equipment and material purchases, and **OPERATING COSTS** to cover things such as rent, fuel and salaries. It is as well that you have evidence for these figures rather than wild guesses.

If your business has several different revenue streams, you should also detail how and when each will bring in money. Remember here to consider the timing of different revenue streams – whether payment is on order, on delivery or on account. Ditto your costs, especially if you are buying and holding stock. This can have a very big impact on your cash flow.

You can enlist the help of an accountant to prepare or review your financial statements, but make sure you understand the content of these documents. Investors and bankers are not impressed by businesspeople who don't understand the financial aspects of their own business!

PROFIT & LOSS STATEMENT

This brings the figures together, telling you the profit or loss for a given period. It is helpful for planning and to help control operating expenses. List projections monthly for the first year and include the information in the points overleaf.

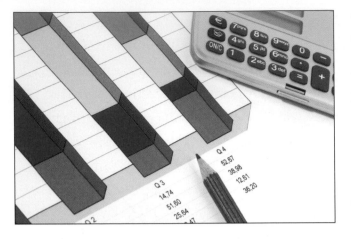

YOU CAN USE GRAPHS AND TABLES *in your business plan to help yourself and others understand your figures. If you don't already use one of the software accounting packages aimed at small businesses, then teach yourself these useful skills at the planning stage.*

1 SALES PROJECTIONS. Number of units sold, the price and therefore the gross revenue.

2 COST OF GOODS/SERVICES. Your cost for manufacturing or buying goods and all other related costs such as packaging, storage etc. This could include subcontractor or casual staff costs.

3 CONTROLLABLE EXPENSES. Every business has its own view of what constitutes a 'controllable' expense. For many it includes salaries and payroll, perks, professional services and advertising.

4 FIXED EXPENSES. These might include rent, loan payments, insurance, licenses and permits.

Once you have these items listed, add 2, 3 & 4 together then deduct them from 1 and you have your Net Profit (or Loss) before taxes.

CASH FLOW STATEMENT

Whilst the profit & loss statement is based on 'commitments' (i.e. invoices and credit accounts) your cash flow statement shows the amounts of cash needed to go out over a period of time, as well as cash that is coming in. Your 'cash flow' covers your cash receipts (such as cash sales, collections from credit sales and remittances) minus your cash disbursements (everything you have paid out during that period). What's left over is your 'net cash flow'. As a start-up, you begin with a Cash Flow Projection. Once you start trading you may want to include another column for your actual figures, which will help you see how realistic your expectations were and to make changes to the way you do business if necessary.

There is more information about business accounting and financial planning in a sister title to this book, called *Dragons' Den: Grow Your Business*.

THE PEOPLE

If your business is a one-person lifestyle business or simple Partnership then this aspect will simply be your CV(s) with a mention of any areas where you will be getting specific advice and help, such as a bookkeeper.

If you are going for something bigger, with staff, you will need to set out your proposed organizational structure showing the skill sets of your people and the necessary resources you will be using to plan, organize, control and deliver your business. You need to show that you have the capacity to develop and build your product or service, manage your finances, market and sell your product/service, oversee your operations and carry out the administration.

SLINKS

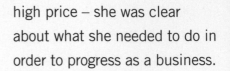

Designer Jane Rafter's visit to the Den was far from plain sailing – fashion is a tricky business with which to woo investors – but her tight control of the numbers in her business plan placed her in good stead. What was most impressive was that – while she was already doing well in having created highly versatile and well-made sandals that she was selling at a high price – she was clear about what she needed to do in order to progress as a business.

Jane was focused on reducing her unit costs and being able to retail her products at a lower price to increase the number of sales and outlets that would stock her shoes. Jane had identified India as the place to move the manufacturing in order to reduce costs by a third, and she had forecast three years of growing turnover and increasing profits.

The only downside was that Jane hadn't accounted for her own salary, which was quite an oversight!

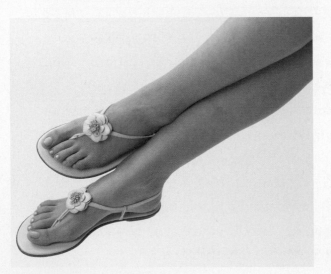

Jane detailed exactly how she would spend the investment, however, allocating portions to improving the range, manufacturing more stock, having a marketing and advertising budget, and pushing to get into specific foreign markets she had targeted.

Jane's planning had proved her to be investable, and she secured a joint offer from Theo and James.

SLINKS' JANE RAFTER *had identified key markets – specifically affluent Mediterranean coastal resorts such as Cannes – where she felt she could increase sales of her sandals. Having now moved production to India, Jane is forging ahead with her marketing and sales plans.*

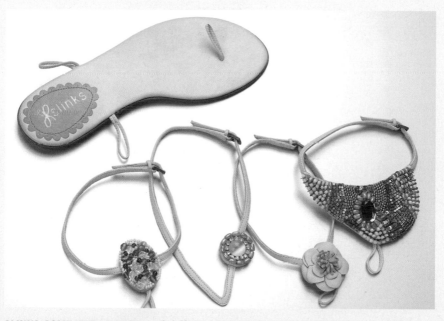

SLINKS COME WITH A BASE *and different design options for the strappy part of the sandals so that the look of the sandals can be quickly changed.*

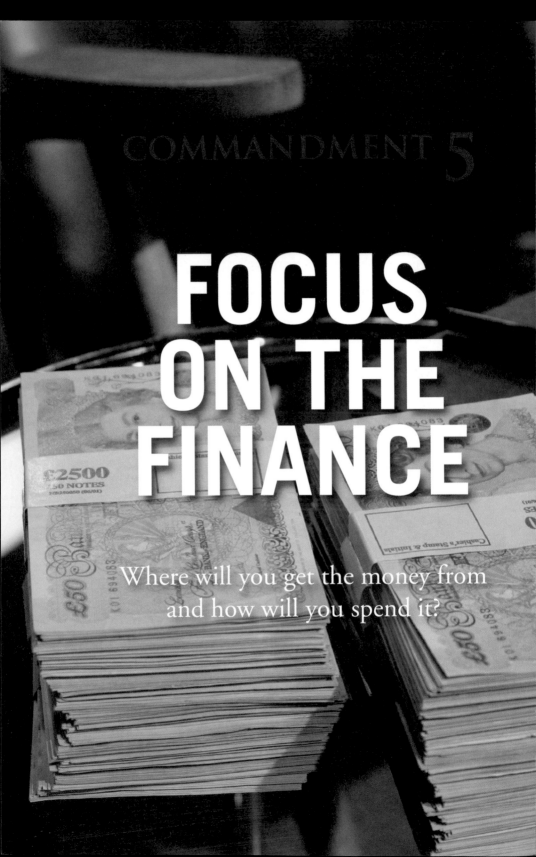

COMMANDMENT 5

FOCUS ON THE FINANCE

Where will you get the money from and how will you spend it?

EVERY BUSINESS EXISTS TO MAKE MONEY. Your principal aim may be simply to do something you enjoy, but you need money to survive, so whatever your motivation for starting your business you have to get this bit right. A chunk of money from private investors is what entrepreneurs are seeking when they go on Dragons' Den, but there are, of course, other channels for funding. This chapter has three main topics: how to secure funds; how to manage money on a day-to-day basis; and how to spend money wisely. There is also an expenditure checklist at the end, which covers the main areas of spending that most start-up business owners need to take into consideration.

Many a start-up business fails before it's even launched because the would-be entrepreneur doesn't have a lump sum and is unable to convince the bank manager or anyone else to lend the money or invest in them.

Your well-constructed business plan (see previous chapter) should go a long way to convince others of the viability of your idea. But you need to be absolutely clear about your financial position and what you really need before you make an appointment with that bank manager or private investor.

KNOW HOW MUCH YOU NEED TO START UP

To assess whether or not you actually need any external funding is the first task. Consider these two crucial areas that start-up businesses nearly always need money for:

1 **CAPITAL EXPENDITURE.** This is the money you need to fork out for tools, equipment, materials, premises, stock, etc. Depending on the type of business, the amount you need will vary dramatically from a few hundred pounds (e.g. some lifestyle businesses can operate from home with the household PC or a few tools bought second-hand) to hundreds of thousands of pounds if you need to lease a factory and tool it up for manufacture.

2 **OPERATING EXPENSES.** You need money to pay for ongoing rent, consumables, salaries, marketing expenses and so on.

RONAN MCCARTHY'S SPIT 'N' POLISH SHOESHINE COMPANY *isn't your average shoeshine stall. Traditionally, this has been a cheap business to set up – brushes, some polish and a box on which a customer can place a shoe. The Spit 'n' Polish booth costs £5,400 to build and comes complete with paper racks, mobile phone charge points and on-screen advertising (see pp134–5).*

When you look at operating expenses you will need to factor into your calculations a realistic expectation of the lead time between starting the business and receiving your first payments from customers or clients. An important factor in lead time is the payment style that commonly applies your industry. For example, is the norm to receive cash on completion; stage payments made with debit/credit cards; invoicing on 30 days, 60 days or 90 days; or monthly standing order?

Here are two examples of small business start-ups with very different capital expenditures, operating expenses, payment styles and lead times:

JOE BLOGGS WINDOW CLEANERS

CAPITAL EXPENDITURE: Ladder, bucket, handcart, overalls

OPERATING EXPENSES: 500 x business cards, cleaning cloths, Joe's personal income requirements

PAYMENT STYLE: Cash on completion

LEAD TIME: Potentially a couple of hours, as the plan is to knock on doors and make an immediate offer of work or leave a card

START-UP COSTS: £250

JOSEPH PUBLIC WEB DESIGN

CAPITAL EXPENDITURE: 2 x top-of-the-range AppleMacs; printer and latest software; deposit on a serviced office

OPERATING EXPENSES: Advertising campaign, mobile phone and internet costs, rent of serviced office, contents insurance, business cards and stationery, design supplies, image fees, accountancy and banking fees, an assistant's salary, Joseph's personal income requirements

PAYMENT STYLE: 60 days from submission of invoices

LEAD TIME: Potentially three months to first commission, plus two months to completion of first project, plus 60 days to payment of first invoice

START-UP COSTS: £15,000 capital expenditure, plus £25,000 for six months' operating expenses including assistant's salary, plus £15,000 for Joseph's personal living costs for first six months – total £55,000

Joseph's web design business requires more than 200 times the start-up costs of Joe's window cleaning business owing to the higher capital expenditure and operating costs, and longer lead times.

Work out your own needs for capital and operating costs, factor in the lead times and calculate how much money you need to set up your business.

SECURING THE FUNDS

Some entrepreneurs have a lump sum of their own that they use to start up their business. For example, savings, an inheritance, a sale of assets, a win on the lottery. If the lump sum covers the start-up costs then it saves the extra effort, expense and strings attached when you need to secure and service funds from an external source.

However, don't skip the business plan and calculations of start-up costs just because you don't need to convince investors about your business idea. You don't want to throw your own money down the drain on a weak business idea. Moreover, you may well also find that you need to secure extra funds on top of your own lump sum in order to start up, especially if you need lots of equipment and stock, lead times are long, and you need to employ other people.

Over the next few pages, we will look at the usual sources of business funding.

BUSINESS LOANS

Many financial services organizations offer business loans. Most of the UK's high street banks will consider an application for a business loan as well as offering business banking facilities. A loan source might also be found from private individuals, which might include family members or friends.

Anyone who is going to lend you money has two fundamental concerns. Are you going to be able to repay their capital and interest? And what can they do to recover their money if you can't?

"AN ENTREPRENEUR IN DEBT IS AN ENTREPRENEUR IN BUSINESS"

DUNCAN BANNATYNE, DRAGON

A lender, whether it is the bank manager or a friend or family member, may well ask for 'security' or 'collateral'. In many cases the security asked for is your house! Fundamentally this means that if you default on the loan repayments they can take your house, sell it and give you back the difference between what you owe them and what they sold the house for. This may be more than the amount you borrowed plus interest; it will undoubtedly include a penalty and their costs of marketing and conveyancing the house.

Many lenders are happy to take 'guarantor' security; they can accept a third party as a guarantor of the repayment. In practice, this may mean that the guarantor offers their house as security against the loan. This is usually sought when the business principal is a son or daughter and the parents are guaranteeing the loan because the principal has no foot on the property ladder.

If you enter into a loan agreement with a family member, then both parties need to be aware of the potential implications both on family relationships between lender and borrower and possible issues due to the perception of the matter in the minds of other family members (e.g. are you borrowing/risking *my* inheritance?).

SAMANTHA FOUNTAIN *wrote a business plan in 2003 that worked out exactly how much money was needed to make her Shewee business a success: the sum was £120,000. "I decided to sell shares in the business. I sent my business plan to over 300 people – hard copies and emailed versions to everyone and anyone! I put a deadline of six months to receive interest from anyone who might like to invest. On the deadline, I received £80,000. I later raised the final amount. I have sold 49% of the shares in total (see also p147).*

- **PROS OF BUSINESS LOANS.** Loans are normally easier to get than investment. There are more sources of loan funding than virtually any other option. A loan is finite – once it is paid off the business is yours alone. A loan is for a fixed period – so long as you keep up the repayments you know it is there.

- **CONS OF BUSINESS LOANS.** Interest payments and charges can be crippling to a start-up. If you offer everything as security then the business becomes life critical – if the business fails you lose your house, which can be an especially bad situation if you have a family to support!

TANGLE TEEZER

Hair colourist Shaun Pulfrey ventured into the Dragons' Den in 2007. As a product-driven business, though, it isn't a business until the first sales are made and one can gauge how the market is responding. For this reason, his pitch in the Den was a case of unfortunate timing – for the Dragons at least. Shaun came away without the investment he was looking for, but his online sales soon began to take off. Up to this point, Shaun had operated as a Sole Trader, but now it was time to formalize a business. He did this and took out a director's loan of nearly £100,000 to pay for the start-up production costs. With sufficient stock levels and a groundswell of endorsements for the Tangle Teezer, Shaun was able to take the product into the high street. It was launched in 200 Boots stores in late 2008, and within a year it had sold more than 30,000 units, exceeding forecasts by almost 50%. As a result, since April 2010, it has been put into 560 stores, and the range has been expanded.

ONE OF THE LATEST PRODUCTS
in the Tangle Teezer range is a child's flower pot brush.

SHAUN PULFREY FIRST HAD THE IDEA OF HIS TANGLE TEEZER HAIRBRUSH *in the mid-1990s, but didn't start to make working prototypes until 2004. He remortgaged his flat to pay for part of the development costs and finally had a product ready to go to market in 2007. He subsequently took out a director's loan from the bank to start his company. As profits rose quickly, he was soon able to repay the loan, and so he's very glad he didn't go down the road of giving equity in exchange for investment.*

BUSINESS GRANTS

Whereas you have to repay a loan along with interest, a grant is a gift… it is not repayable. But grants usually have two caveats – one is that you will need to qualify for something to receive the grant (e.g. the Prince's Trust will grant money only to people of a certain age group), and the other is that strings usually relate to the use of the money (e.g. only for capital equipment or only for relevant training) and to reporting its usage. The website www.bizhelp24.com has some useful sources of grants.

- **PROS OF BUSINESS GRANTS:** You don't have to provide security. You don't have to repay the capital. No interest is accruing / repayable.

- **CONS OF BUSINESS GRANTS:** They are hard to get. They are usually limited to a relatively small amount. You lose your independence and have to comply with certain conditions.

SELLING EQUITY TO INVESTORS

This of course is the territory of the Dragons' Den. An investor 'buys' the right to a given percentage of your profits in return for cash to cover what you need to set up.

The investor may be an active partner, with whom you share the risks, the rewards and the workload equitably, or the investor may be less active, showing up only occasionally to see what you are up to but taking no share of the work. It is really important to have a clear agreement about these matters before you start.

You can sell equity to what is sometimes jokingly called the 'FFF market' – Family, Friends and Fools – people who have a few thousand to invest in the business. Normally they are not able to afford a big risk and are not looking for an enormous return but they don't usually bring anything to the table either.

You can sell equity to a 'business angel' (maybe one of those Dragons!). Business angels generally have much more money to invest and are prepared to take a bigger risk, but they are looking for much bigger returns and usually a clearly very profitable exit strategy (such as a saleable company or a flotation).

- **PROS OF SELLING EQUITY TO INVESTORS:** The money you're given doesn't accrue

STEVE SMITH PRESENTED TRUECALL *to the Dragons in Series 7 (see p103). He had a good product and a sound business plan to sell units whilst approaching phone manufacturers with a view to ultimately incorporating his technology in their handsets. Combined with his proven business track record, this led to Steve releasing only a relatively small amount of equity (12.5%) for £100,000 investment.*

ANDY HARSLEY'S CASE WITH RAPSTRAP *(see pp196–7) was a bit different. Again, he had a good product, but he needed more input from the Dragons in order to turn his invention into a business with global distribution. They had the contacts and the investment would provide the funds to start mass production of the Rapstrap. For these reasons it made sense to part with far more equity (50%).*

any interest and therefore no extra monthly outgoings. As in Dragons' Den, the money may come with the expertise/reputation of the investor attached. You aren't risking your home.

- **CONS OF SELLING EQUITY TO AN INVESTOR:** It's a long-term commitment; the investor is now firmly involved in your business and will want to know, and have a say in, what you are spending his or her money on.

Technically it isn't a 'con' of selling equity, but bear in mind that if the business really takes off you could find yourself with someone who owns half of your multi-million-pound company in return for having loaned you a couple of thousand… granted you own the other half, so it isn't as though you are hard up, but it might rankle!

USING CREDIT FACILITIES IN BUSINESS

Credit accounts – with which you can delay payment for goods or services for a month or more – are a good way to ease cash flow, but will be limited to certain suppliers (see the point about 'lead times' on pp115–17). If you default on a credit account you lose a potentially valuable supplier. (Would you keep supplying someone who never pays?) Many suppliers run their own unofficial 'blacklist'.

Credit cards are a tempting way to operate, particularly with a small business where you anticipate or hope for a quick income, but the interest rates are typically astronomical in comparison to a business loan, and credit card companies are quick to hand out poor credit scores.

Overdrafts offer the benefit of being quick and sometimes personal to set up. They are convenient in that they are directly linked to your current account, out of which most of your funds go. The downsides of an overdraft are costs (interest and fees) and that they are usually 'discretionary' – they can be recalled

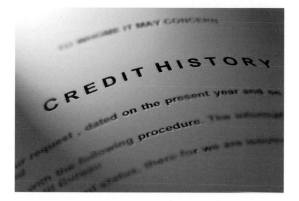

CREDIT RATING AGENCIES *such as Experian in the UK hold data about the credit history of companies. You can check the status of your clients – do they have a history of defaulting? – and they can check your status.*

with virtually no notice and for no specific reason. Banks have been known to suddenly foreclose on all business overdrafts in order to reduce their market exposure to risk in certain parts of the economy.

OPENING A BUSINESS BANK ACCOUNT

Even if your business is very small and you don't need a bank loan, it is recommended that you open a business current account to keep your business transactions separate from your personal current account transactions. It is also a good idea to open at least one other account for VAT, tax and other funds that need to be kept aside.

If this is your first business, your bank manager will probably want to see your business plan and have a personal discussion when you apply for a business account (even if you are not applying for a business loan). Laws to prevent money laundering in the UK have been tightened in recent years, and you will have to undergo a number of identity and security checks to open the account.

THE COST OF BUSINESS TRANSACTIONS

It comes as a surprise to many new entrepreneurs that business transactions usually incur bank charges, whereas their personal bank transactions are free!

Some banks waive some of their business banking charges in the first year or two of a business as an incentive, but you must still factor in the cost of business banking when planning and setting the price of your goods or services. The charges that apply to handling cash and cheques rather than using direct debits and standing orders – e.g. 70p for every cheque paid in – can have a significant impact on profit margins for some businesses.

If you plan to offer your customers the option to pay by debit or credit card then you will also need to factor in the cost of the card-reading equipment and the differing percentages charged by the banks, credit card companies and online banking service companies for each transaction.

MANAGING MONEY DAY-TO-DAY

Before you start up you should look for an accountant who can offer advice, handle your tax affairs and prepare your annual returns. Accountancy fees are part of your operating expenses.

Accountants working for small businesses generally are not employed to keep the records of day-to-day transactions – that's your job. No matter how much you hate doing accounts, you have got to keep good records of your financial activity. The image of the small businessperson putting all the receipts in a shoebox is not one to be copied; you will end up either in trouble with the HMRC or paying a lot of money to an accountant to do something that you could have done yourself for little effort. It's fine to employ a part-time bookkeeper for the task though, so long as you yourself understand the books and cash flow situation at any given time.

The complexity of your accounting procedures will depend on the complexity and size of your business. Whether you buy a specialist accounts package, use a standard spreadsheet or keep your books literally will be dictated by the circumstances. But there are five fundamental rules that all businesses should follow, which we'll summarize here:

1 **KEEP AN ACCURATE RECORD OF SALES.** Be they credit or cash, large or small, subject to VAT or not, all sales transactions need to be recorded.

2 **KEEP AN ACCURATE RECORD OF ALL EXPENDITURE.** This includes purchases you might have made on a personal account and need to reimburse from business funds. You need to keep all the evidence – invoices, receipts etc.

3 **MAINTAIN STRICT CREDIT CONTROL PROCEDURES.** Set up and adhere to systems for invoicing your customers and clients, e.g. on 30 days' credit. Likewise for your expenditure, know what you have to pay on which date.

4 **KNOW YOUR DEBTORS AND HOW MUCH THEY OWE.** It's easy for time to slip by while your clients claim that "payment is in the post" or make themselves hard to pin down. Chasing payment is a major activity for many businesses.

5 **ALWAYS RECONCILE THE BOOKS WITH THE BANK ACCOUNT.** Whenever you update the accounts, be it daily or weekly, always ensure that the balance in the bank is

the same as the balance in your books (minus any transactions recorded in the books but not yet showing up in the bank account). If they're not exactly the same figure, then you've made an error that needs to be identified.

WHY YOU NEED TO KEEP ON TOP OF YOUR ACCOUNTS

Always being in control of your business accounts will prevent surprises. Here are some good reasons why you need to keep records and stay on top of your transactions in the way described above:

... **BECAUSE OF HER MAJESTY'S REVENUE & CUSTOMS.** The HMRC is the official reason why you need to keep accurate records. It will want to know (and can demand to know) how much you have billed and received.

... **BECAUSE YOU OWE IT TO YOUR STAFF.** If you employ staff you always need adequate funds to cover their salaries, and you are also obliged to ensure accurate deduction and payment of NI contributions and PAYE tax.

... **BECAUSE OF YOUR VAT STATUS.** If your turnover reaches the threshold where you must register for and charge VAT you need to do this in advance otherwise you will find yourself having to pay VAT you haven't received. You also need to keep the records of VAT paid out so you can claim back everything that you are allowed to.

... **BECAUSE OF THE QUARTERLY AND ANNUAL RETURNS.** You are more likely to have adequate funds set aside for your VAT or other tax if you keep on top of your books throughout the year.

... **BECAUSE YOU DON'T WANT TO PAY MORE TAX THAN YOU NEED TO.** In order not to pay too much in tax you need to prove what your business's outgoings are, and you can't do that without keeping records.

... **BECAUSE YOU NEED TO KNOW HOW MUCH TO SELL IN ORDER TO KEEP TRADING.** Anticipating your ongoing monthly costs will help you set realistic targets for sales.

... **BECAUSE YOU MAY NEED TO CHASE PEOPLE WHO OWE YOU.** Late-paying customers (and non-paying customers) are one of the biggest causes of small businesses going bust. If a customer goes bust owing you money you are unlikely to ever see the full value of what they owe, regardless of what it cost you to deliver the service to them.

... **BECAUSE YOU DON'T WANT TO SLIP ACCIDENTALLY INTO THE RED.** It's not pleasant having to tell the bank manager that you are sorry you have exceeded your limit, or explaining to your creditors why your cheque bounced.

It is a really good idea to speak with your local Business Link (go to www.businesslink.gov.uk) or a local accountant about how to set up your accounting procedures.

SPENDING WISELY

It is easy to get carried away when you are setting up a business, especially if you have just got a loan or investment capital and it looks as if cash is free and easy. However, it is important to take a cold hard approach to make sure everything you spend money on is a genuine 'investment', i.e. that you are going to get an appropriate return on the outlay. This ranges from people (are you employing your brother simply because you can or is he actually better than any other employee?), to premises (is there a calculable benefit in having a Central London office or could we do just as well with a cheaper unit in the suburbs?), to equipment (are we going to use that expensive tool enough to justify buying one or are we better served renting one as and when we need it?), to development (do I really need to enrol in a £16,500+VAT Advanced Management Programme at a top UK Business School or should I just buy the rest of the books in this series?).

What you need to do with any proposed expenditure is to carry out a cost/benefit analysis. You probably do this anyway with pretty much everything you buy. Weigh up what it is going to cost against the benefit it is going to bring.

In the cost element, remember to consider the cost of ownership, not just the price on the sticker. For example, what the company car costs to insure, tax, service, store and run. You also need to consider depreciation; if you buy a new car it loses a percentage of its value as you drive it off the forecourt. Depreciation is a 'cost' that you can offset against tax.

In the benefit element, remember that there are some benefits that may be less easy to see; for example that Advanced Management Programme may allow you to rub shoulders with prospective clients, so it has a networking benefit to the marketing of your service.

EXPENDITURE CHECKLIST

Obviously every business is different and has its own expenditure breakdown. However, most businesses need to spend in certain areas, so here is a checklist for you to take into consideration.

✔ **PEOPLE:** Your employees, other directors and yourself are usually the main source of spending for any business. Don't forget to allow for employer's NI as a percentage on top of gross wages (see p71). Check on the latest tax implications of employee benefits such as company cars, company health schemes and company pensions. Include expenses such as for business trips and business lunches. Understand and accept that your employees may make more money from your venture in its infancy than you do yourself. (And sadly, some entrepreneurs only ever build up debts from their venture.)

✔ **DIRECT COSTS:** Your *direct costs* are those you incur in providing your goods or service. That might include manufacturing, distribution, marketing, advertising, mailing costs… the list will be specific to your industry and likely to have many items on it!

✔ **PREMISES:** This is often regarded as the main element of your *indirect costs*, or *overheads*. As well as the basic cost of rent, remember to include the cost of utilities such as electricity, heating, water, broadband and telecommunications. Also check the business rates for the premises, which are set by and paid to the Local Authority. Allow funds for cleaning and maintenance, and health and safety features. Serviced offices, which are popular with small start-ups, will include some but not necessarily all of these extra elements.

✔ **EQUIPMENT AND FURNITURE:** Some equipment will be part of your direct costs; some may be for overheads – e.g. a printer. You might want to include stationery and other office consumables here.

✔ **INSURANCE:** The cost of Contents Insurance will vary dramatically according to your line of business. Insurers are likely to insist on expensive security equipment and complex procedures if your equipment and stock are particularly valuable. You may also need Employers' Liability Insurance, Public Liability Insurance and Professional Indemnity Insurance (see pp85–6).

✔ **SOLICITOR:** You may well need to use a solicitor's services when starting up a business and ongoing, and they tend not to come cheap.

✔ **ACCOUNTANT:** A good accountant will help you run an efficient business and provide ongoing support, but will need paying too!

✔ **BANK CHARGES AND INTEREST:** On any business loans or overdrafts.

✔ **LOGO, STATIONERY AND WEBSITE DESIGN:** You need an identity from the moment you start up a business.

✔ **SUBSCRIPTIONS AND REFERENCE:** This might include membership to trade organizations and training manuals.

✔ **TAX:** Never forget about this major element! See pp69–80. Set aside a proportion of funds each quarter in anticipation of your likely tax bill at the end of your accounting year.

SPIT 'N' POLISH SHOESHINE

Ronan McCarthy went into the Den in Series 7, looking for £108,000 for 10% equity in his modern take on an old-fashioned shoeshine booth.

RONAN BEGAN HIS PITCH *whilst having his shoes polished to demonstrate the product.*

In Ronan's smart 21st-century version, the booth would have a screen for displaying advertising, a selection of newspapers and a mobile phone charging socket. The plan was to put the booths into transport hubs such as airports and railway stations.

Ronan had been working on the project for 18 months and had already secured some investment and his first two locations: Heathrow and Stansted. The investment he was now seeking was in order to roll out the booths, which cost him £5,400 to build, in 10 locations. He gave impressive figures for operating profits over a three-year period, but his figures were dependent on an average of seven customers per hour, and none of the Dragons thought this likely. However, James Caan thought that, even if there were fewer customers, a good profit was still possible. He did want 40% of the equity, though, and Ronan thought this was far too much.

With Ronan unwilling to negotiate further, James withdrew his offer. As Theo pointed out, it could have been a very different story if Ronan had gone to the Den having already got the business under-way with at least one shoeshine booth in operation. He could then have backed up his figures with facts, but, as it was, his figures were too speculative to convince the Dragons.

The lesson is really that investors are cautious and, if you want a large amount of investment in a business venture that is embryonic and has no track record to give it credence, you'll have to be prepared to give up a large amount of equity. Ronan wasn't prepared to do this, and so the deal faltered.

DEBORAH BECAME FRUSTRATED *as she tried to elicit the projected turnover and profit figures; Ronan wanted to proffer a different set of figures, based on the number of customers per hour and the price of each shoeshine.*

WITH HIS SHOES FRESHLY SHINED *James was ready to make an offer – not one that Ronan was prepared to accept, however, as he saw his business as low maintenance for a Dragon.*

MAKE YOUR MARK WITH MARKETING

Who do you want to appeal to and how
will you go about wooing them?

LET'S BE CLEAR, MARKETING AND SELLING ARE TWO DIFFERENT THINGS. The Chartered Institute of Marketing defines marketing as: 'The management process responsible for identifying, anticipating and satisfying customer requirements profitably.' Whereas selling is usually defined as: 'The exchange of goods or services for an agreed price.' So, whilst selling is part of marketing, marketing is a lot more than selling. You need to be clear about your market before setting up in business. Know who you need to target, create a brand for your business, get some publicity, get on the internet and get yourself out there in the marketplace.

You have already been introduced to the 'Marketing Mix' in Commandment 4 – the four 'P's of Position, Price, Promotion and Place. We'll look at these 'P's in detail in this chapter.

P = POSITION

Based on your research, you need to decide how you are going to position your product or service.

- A **PREMIUM BRAND** – exclusive, expensive and aspirational – can only work if there really is a differentiator between it and the economy market place. It can only work if there are customers who both want, and are able to pay the price for, that product and service.

MOTORMOUSE APPEARED IN SERIES 7. *The product is a wireless computer mouse, superbly made as a series of replica classic sports cars. Because the detailing is so much better than any comparable product, the company's directors, David and Patti Bailey, felt confident in positioning the mouse as a premium brand and pricing it accordingly.*

- A **MIDDLE-OF-THE-ROAD BRAND** will have to fight to stand out from the crowd and will be forever trying to differentiate itself from a large field of competitors, but having done so usually retains loyal following.

- An **ECONOMY BRAND** is always going to be price sensitive.

P = PRICE

Again based on the outcomes of your research, you have to determine your pricing structure. The less you have to differentiate on price the better, because generally speaking if price is all that separates you from the competition, your customers will defect in droves if someone undercuts you. Traditionally if you are competing heavily on price your margins are small, so any reduction (to combat undercutting) can easily push you into a state where you are trading at a loss.

P = PROMOTION

There is an acronym, **AIDA**, which has been coined to summarize the four 'stages' of the promotional cycle – the potential 'objectives' of each promotional act:

- **AWARENESS OR ATTENTION**
- **INTEREST**
- **DESIRE**
- **ACTION**

NEUROTICA

When fashion designer Victoria McGrane went into the Den she wanted to extend her market reach. She had been in business for about a year, and was currently selling limited edition high-end clothing into a handful of boutiques in the UK, Japan and the States. Now she wanted investment to create a more mass-market range, Neurotica White Label, for selling into high street shops.

VICTORIA SPEAKING ABOUT NEUROTICA *in the Den.*

The £56,000 investment she was hoping to obtain would be partly used for producing the new White Label range and partly for marketing in order to launch the range properly. That would mean exhibiting at trade shows and promoting the label at major industry events such as London Fashion Week.

Victoria had realized that to launch anything mainstream would require considerably more marketing input than the high-end, low-volume sector, and the stakes in terms of stock value would be much higher. Peter Jones thought she wasn't asking for enough money for a successful marketing strategy. He offered £75,000 instead, for 35% equity in the business, which Victoria gladly accepted.

AFTER RECEIVING INVESTMENT *from Peter Jones, Victoria soon launched the Neurotica White Label diffusion range in Topshop. In practice, however, she found that buyers wanted to order items across both ranges and so the distinction of the White and Black labels became less significant. In response to the buyers' inclinations, Victoria has consolidated her designs into one range, rather than splitting the buyers' attention. Unique prints have always been the primary focus of Neurotica's designs, more so than fabrics and tailoring, and Victoria now produces some lower cost items such as T-shirts to create some higher unit sales and increase Neurotica's market presence. With a consolidated range, the marketing can be more streamlined too.*

SAMMY FRENCH'S FIT FUR LIFE *business got a new lease of life once James Caan was on board. The first thing James's team did was to update the website with a video demonstration of Sammy's product, a treadmill for dogs. That meant Sammy no longer had to spend so much time travelling to demonstrate the model and could concentrate more effectively on sales and marketing in a wider context. Promoting the product at dog shows is still important, of course, and Fit Fur Life now has a team of colleagues that attends various trade and consumer exhibitions in the UK. Overseas orders have also taken off, and so a distributor has been appointed in Australia.*

STAGE 1 OF AIDA – AWARENESS OR ATTENTION

You need to draw attention to or create awareness of your product or service. People will not buy from you if they don't know you are there or don't know what you do.

One critical area of this is the matter of your business's trading name or website name; it can be argued that there is little value in splashing *Steve Smith* on the side of your van if no one knows what Steve Smith does. Whereas an advert in a trade magazine that says *Smith's Widget Warehouse – www.smithswidgets.co.uk –* could be an effective way to create awareness of the business's existence and area of expertise.

A small 'puff' in the local paper that Julie Jackson is starting a restoration business, based on her 10 years' experience of restoration at Tottington Hall will create some awareness. (A 'puff' isn't a paid-for advert but a small article; local businesses can often get great mileage out of local papers who are often very keen on local items.) The music coming from an ice-cream van is an example of something that creates awareness of a temporary shop. A banner slung from the scaffolding on a pub that says *Closed for Refurbishment* creates awareness that the pub is going to re-open in a changed style. 'Less-is-more' is often the watchword of promotional activity that simply aims to create attention or awareness.

" WHEN I SET UP MY PRIVATE EQUITY FIRM, I WAS SITTING IN THE KITCHEN THINKING WHAT SORT OF BUSINESS WILL THIS BE? THE IMAGE OF THE BRADFORD & BINGLEY LOGO, WITH THE TWO GUYS IN THE BOWLER HAT, SPRANG TO MIND. WHEN YOU'RE DEALING WITH MONEY IT'S ABOUT BEING ESTABLISHED, BEING SAFE, HAVING INTEGRITY. I THOUGHT ONE SHOULD BE CALLED HAMILTON AND ONE BRADSHAW. "

JAMES CAAN, DRAGON

STAGE 2 OF AIDA – INTEREST

You want to generate some interest in your product or service. This still doesn't mean telling your target audience everything about it, but you give enough to make them want to know more about it. Signs that say *SALE* or *To Let* are common examples. TV adverts that tell you nothing about the actual car but show it in soft focus driving through exploding sugar fields driven by beautiful, mysterious people aim to create interest.

Some companies use 'teasers' leading up to the advert; the teaser tells you nothing but keeps you guessing… "I wonder what on earth this is an advert for?"

SARAH LU'S YOUDOO DOLL *featured in Series 5 (see also p209). To create a buzz around the product and to give consumers a sense of having joined a club, the doll has its own website, which continues the homemade fun aesthetic of the doll itself. The site allows customers to upload images of their unique dolls to an evolving gallery, and there are regular bulletins of events and Sarah's blog to keep it looking fresh. As more products have been developed, such as Youdoo Pets and Youdoo Superheroes, distinct websites have been created for those toys too.*

The message at this point is often fairly generic; aimed at the segment of the market but not necessarily the individual buyer. This is the point where the prospective customer's interest is piqued enough to visit your shop, make an appointment or call you.

STAGE 3 OF AIDA – DESIRE

Whereas 'interest' created a desire to know more about the product or service, now you want to create a desire to own or buy the product or service. Now the message is more personal: you are trying to find which features of your product or service would present specific benefits to your prospective customer and you are telling the prospective client about those benefits.

If you are selling a service, this is probably the point where you are interacting directly with the customer. You might be talking to them on the doorstep of their home, if you are a B2C (business-to-consumer) business such as domestic products or services; or their office if your business is a B2B (business-to-business) service such as web design or office catering; or at the shop counter if you are in the retail sector.

STAGE 4 OF AIDA – ACTION

Converting desire into action is the goal of every salesperson. Until the customer actually buys your product or service you are not making money. Promotional activity that aims to achieve a sale is usually intensely personalized.

If your business is a high-value service or product, achieving action may require several meetings and be very labour intensive and costly (for example it is not unusual for professional firms to spend £10,000 in pursuing one tender). In this instance it is critical that your promotional activity is directed at the 'MAN'… which stands for the person with the Money, the Authority and the Need.

With a low-cost service or product, the purchase may be almost an impulse buy and therefore require little input from you.

BRINGING AIDA TO LIFE

Whether you are out to create awareness, generate interest or stimulate desire, there are many ways to get the message across. Some are expensive in time and money (e.g. one appearance of a

20cm x 2-column advert in the *Daily Mail* letters page Monday to Wednesday will cost more than £7,000 with VAT) and some almost free (e.g. Twitter, more of which in a bit).

When looking at media to spread your message, consider the whole range:

- TV, radio, magazines, national and local press
- Press releases and 'puffs'
- Trade press and trade exhibitions
- Posters and hoardings
- The livery of your company vehicles and building
- Your work-wear
- Your own website, email, blog
- Direct mailings
- Social networking sites
- Your family and friends

Whatever your line of business, you should exploit the power of online media to the full. That includes having your own website (more below), getting yourself into online directories and using online advertising methods such as Google AdWords.

" I DON'T THINK YOU CAN BE A PROPER CITIZEN OF OUR SOCIETY IN THE FUTURE IF YOU ARE NOT ENGAGED ONLINE " MARTHA LANE FOX, FOUNDER OF LASTMINUTE.COM AND CHAMPION FOR DIGITAL INCLUSION

SHEWEE

Samantha Fountain appeared in Series 2 of the Den with her memorable product Shewee. This carefully shaped plastic funnel for enabling women to urinate while standing up was such an unusual item that it attracted a great amount of media interest from magazines, papers and radio and television.

THOUGH SAMANTHA WASN'T INITIALLY KEEN *to sell via the internet, the advice she was given by the Dragons was to do precisely that.*

This was a boon for marketing, as Samantha explains: "When we first launched the product, we didn't need to push for the articles – the magazines for the 'outdoor' world and 'disability' market loved it. We sent press releases and free samples and they just wrote about this novel idea – it was brilliant!"

This proved valuable for getting the ball rolling, but eventually a more typically businesslike approach to marketing needed to take over, and Samantha's company now spends about £3,000 a month on marketing. She sells through high street shops, outward-bound type websites and in the health sector. The UK, New Zealand and Australian markets have all embraced the Shewee and since 2007 Shewee's turnover has grown from £120,000 to £220,000.

GET ONLINE, GET NETWORKING – *it's essential in today's business world.*

Never underestimate the power of networking and contacts. The old saying "it isn't what you know; it is who you know" is as true today as it ever was. Whether you're on the playing fields of Eton, in the pub or online, your networking opportunities are very powerful. Consider the expansion of the satellite dish. Did it start in upper middle-income homes? No, it started on council housing estates; neighbours spoke over the fence and told their neighbours, who passed it on.

Satisfied customers are potentially your best salespeople. If you can get each paying client to recommend two friends, and one of them becomes a paying customer, you are successfully 'selling'. In a high-value market you may spend six months getting one client, but if that client brings you one more recommended client, that saves six months. In a commodity market, one client may take one week to win, so one recommendation is one week saved.

GET A WEB PRESENCE

Don't even think about launching a business in the UK in the 2010s without a website. According to the Office for National Statistics, 18.3 million households in the UK (70%) had internet access in 2009. This was an increase of just under 2 million households (11%)

over the last year. Even Scotland, with the lowest density of online homes, was 62%. So in the B2C (business-to-consumer) marketplace, 60–70% of your prospective customers will search for you or look you up on the web. If you are in the B2B (business-to-business) market, it is probably 99.9% of your prospective customers!

Websites are not necessarily expensive or complicated. You can buy a 'website-in-a-box' for less than £50 for a whole year. Your website creates a market image for you 24 hours a day, and may generate income for you even whilst you sleep. You can add your website link to local internet listings, often for much less outlay than a listing in a printed directory.

TWITTERING *at 140 characters per tweet*

If your business itself is web-based – an internet shop for example – you will need to invest more in your website, putting in robust e-commerce facilities, optimizing it for search engines and different browsers, and employing skilled designers to make it appealing, easy to navigate and stand out from the crowd.

TWITTERING AND BLOGGING

In the modern world it is possible to successfully promote a product or service without ever buying an advert, putting up a poster or mailing a letter. Twitter (http://twitter.com) costs virtually nothing, yet

" SUDDENLY, IT SEEMS AS THOUGH ALL THE WORLD'S A-TWITTER "

NEWSWEEK

many small businesses report that their tweets regularly get them enquiries and lead to paying business. If you tweet a message to 50 followers and 10% of them re-tweet your message to their 50 followers, your tweet will hit 300 people in a matter of seconds... for virtually no cost. Mike Morrison of Rapid Business Improvement has posted 50 tips about using Twitter (http://rapidbi.com).

Tweets are limited to 140 characters and are text only. By contrast, with a blog – which could either be attached to your company website or kept separate with its own keywords – the world is your oyster. Even before setting up a fully-fledged business, entrepreneurs can use blogs to update potential clients about what they are doing and generate interest in new ideas and products. Type 'blog template' into a search engine if you are not sure where to begin.

You can use Twitter to send people to your blog, and your blog to build followers for your tweets.

P = PLACE

Going back to the 'Ps' of the Marketing Mix, the final P is 'Place' – the physical way you are going to take your business to the market. Again you need to listen to your market research. You may then follow the industry norms, which is safe but competitive, or break the mould. To give an example from the real world: if you were selling fertilized chicken eggs to people who want to raise chickens

THE EGLU *is an innovative product that taps into the renewed interest in chicken-keeping in the UK today.*

themselves, you'd expect the norm to be for customers to visit your farm and collect. But nowadays, customers can order online and have the eggs delivered by courier in insulated and shockproof containers. Chicken-keeping is reported to be the fastest growing hobby in the UK, and the small business set up by a group of design students to market their plastic 'Eglu' chicken house (see above) sold 11,000 units at £400 each in their first three years.

BRANDING YOUR BUSINESS

The branding of your business is the initial image you put in the marketplace. It can cover all the following elements:

- **THE CHOSEN NAME OF YOUR BUSINESS OR PRODUCT.**
  Pick a name that is memorable but easy to spell, has a logical and positive connotation about the product or service on offer, is fairly short (even if that means that you shorten it to initials, like Qantas – Queensland And Northern Territory Aerial Service).

- **THE TYPEFACE IN WHICH THE BRAND NAME APPEARS.**
  Think of the long-lived and instantly identifiable
  typefaces of Kellogg's or Harrods. Also choose and use a
  single set of fonts in all your correspondence and
  documentation.

- **LOGO.** It doesn't necessarily take a marketing consultancy
  and millions of pounds to come up with a good logo.
  What you should aim for is a simple shape and colours
  that photocopy, reduce and reproduce easily. People
  should be able to recognize your logo from an
  appropriate distance. McDonald's golden arches were
  designed to be seen from a car in good time to allow
  it to pull over for a burger.

- **SLOGAN OR MOTTO.** Go for something that refers to the
  benefit to the customer; Ronseal's "It does exactly what
  it says on the tin" or Avis's "We try harder" are good
  examples.

- **COLOUR SCHEME.** Orange's orange is instantly
  recognizable on a mobile phone; everything Virgin is red.

- **BADGE.** E.g. BMW's blue and white propeller.

- **SHAPE.** Think of the classic Coke bottle.

KAY RUSSELL OF PHYSICOOL, *who emerged victorious from the Den in Series 7, already had a business with a product for treating muscle injuries to horses. She realized that the same technology could be applied to human muscle injuries but that, in order to move into this new market, she would need to brand the product differently. She came up with Physicool for the brand name and set up a new company to market and trade the product in the sports and fitness, and health and nursing markets.*

Once you are established, you start to create a brand experience – the perception of quality (good or bad) that customers and prospective customers link with your brand image. This is discussed further in Commandment 7.

GOLDGENIE

Laban Roomes received praise and a grilling in equal measure in the Den. The Dragons admired Laban's entrepreneurship and geniality, but put him through the mill on the financing of the franchise operation he planned and the investability of his business, then known as Midas Touch.

James Caan, though, is known for investing in people as much as businesses and he clearly saw a great deal of potential in Laban. A deal was struck in the Den.

James soon familiarized himself with the business, suggested a name change from Midas Touch to Goldgenie and proposed postponing the franchise while they concentrated hard on producing and selling key products, such as gold-plated mobile phones and iPods.

Retail then became the core business for a while, until they felt a sufficient foundation had been made to scale the business up and out through franchise opportunities. With 50% of sales going overseas, franchising also became a way to tap further into overseas markets. Goldgenie now has franchises across Europe.

THOUGH HIS AMBITION *is to build up and at some point sell the business, Laban is passionate about Goldgenie and would seek to remain involved, as a consultant, shareholder and brand ambassador.*

As soon as James invested, he persuaded Laban to bring in employees to carry out the gold-plating itself and handle admin and accounts. Laban was then free to concentrate on sales, marketing and generally being the face of Goldgenie.

Part of that role has been to attract celebrity involvement in Goldgenie products, and a range has been developed with gold iPods carrying the signatures of Olympic gold medal-winning sprinter Usain Bolt and UK music star Tinchy Stryder. Part of this range, known as 'Bling with Benefits', allocates a percentage of the sales to charities – Elton John's Aids Foundation has benefited in this way, as has Cancer Research UK through the Bobby Moore signature iPod.

Laban's company was already established and making a decent profit when he stepped into the Den in 2007,

GOLDGENIE'S RANGE *now includes crystal-embedded products, including the Elton John Starburst iPod.*

but since then the business has really developed. It now provides income for many more people, and Goldgenie's income and profits have trebled.

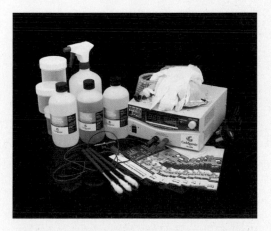

LABAN'S ORIGINAL BUSINESS MODEL *was based on gold-plating with simple, portable electro-chemical equipment.*

PROTECT
AND
SURVIVE

Should you protect your innovation?

YOU NEED LUCK AS WELL AS CREATIVITY to get a truly innovative product or service off the ground. Indeed, some wonderfully inventive ideas have been put before the Dragons over the years, and a lucky few have fired the enthusiasm of the Dragons and received investment, whilst others were perhaps too creative at the expense of a sensible business plan. If your idea does take off, though, you may well need to protect your business because others will soon start copying you. Applying for a patent is time-consuming and costly, but it might be worth the effort if you are granted exclusive rights in your target countries. Other forms of protection include copyright and non-competition clauses in contracts.

The last thing you want is to see all your efforts damaged by someone stealing your ideas, your image and your customers. Imitation may be the highest form of flattery, but flattery doesn't pay the bills!

If your business is based on a tangible product you might be able to patent or copyright your work. Normally an invention (such as a new vacuum cleaner or tool) would be patented, whilst a creation (such as a book, software program, psychometric test, architectural drawing, photograph, painting or song) would be copyrighted. It is possible to patent a process or methodology, but there are complex rules relating to this, which can change with case law. It is best to speak to a patent agent if you are interested in patenting something that you can't actually touch.

Another area that you might want to protect is your image and the revenue you invest in marketing. Designer-orientated companies can spend a fortune creating a brand image of quality and exclusivity, then someone else comes along, creating a 'knock-off' fake version and riding on the coat-tails of the designer brand's investment. Protecting your image and name can also extend to your internet presence. If you propose to do a lot of your business over the web, then you might want to protect the name of your website to prevent loss of business by others using a copycat name. If you work with other people, you can also 'ring-fence' your customers with confidentiality and non-competition contracts to prevent poaching.

This is all complex and costly business, but vital for many businesses. In the UK, the **INTELLECTUAL PROPERTY OFFICE** (www.ipo.gov.uk) manages patents, trademarks and copyrights.

PATENTS

A patent grants exclusive rights by a national government to the inventor for a limited period of time in exchange for a public disclosure of the invention. The exclusive right granted to a patentee in most countries is the right to prevent others from making, using, selling, or distributing your invention without your express written permission. 'Patent agents' are companies that help applicants to obtain patents. The lengthy patenting process in the UK is explained over the next few pages.

1   **BE SECRETIVE.** Don't rush out and tell everyone about your new idea, not even as 'market research'. Tell no one except a patent agent.

2   **FILE A PATENTS FORM AT THE PATENT OFFICE.** You have to submit a description of the invention drafted in accordance with Patent Office rules (you can download a set at www.ipo.gov.uk). This stage is free unless you are also applying for a search (see stage 6).

3 **GET A DATED RECEIPT.** The Patent Office will send you a receipt dating the application, which gives you precedence over the same invention being filed later (it is called a priority date). At this stage, there is no guarantee that the same invention has not already been submitted by someone else.

4 **USE THE ONE-YEAR ASSESSMENT PERIOD.** You now have a year in which to assess whether this invention has wings and to examine the commercial realities, before pressing on with your application. If you don't press on, it will automatically lapse after a year.

5 **FILE A NEW PATENT APPLICATION IF NECESSARY.** If this assessment period leads you to improve your invention, you cannot add the improvement to your first application but must file a new one. However, as long as you do this within a year of the priority date, that date will apply so long as the two are clearly linked. You can then let your first application lapse.

6 **REQUEST A PRELIMINARY SEARCH AND EXAMINATION.** If you want to pursue the patent application you need (within the year from the priority date) to file a request for a preliminary search and examination. At this stage there is a fee to pay. You will also need to file the 'claims' you want on the patent, which define the type of monopoly you are seeking.

" I NEVER PERFECTED AN INVENTION THAT I DID NOT THINK ABOUT IN TERMS OF THE SERVICE IT MIGHT GIVE OTHERS... I FIND OUT WHAT THE WORLD NEEDS, THEN I PROCEED TO INVENT. "

THOMAS EDISON (1847–1931),
INVENTOR OF THE LIGHT BULB

7 **WAIT FOR THE PATENT OFFICE EXAMINER'S SEARCH REPORT.**
An Examiner will then carry out a preliminary search and issue a search report. This is an assessment to compare your invention with others and it is indicative of whether your application is likely to be successful.

8 **HAVE YOUR APPLICATION PUBLISHED BY THE THE PATENT OFFICE.** Unless you decide to withdraw your application at this stage, it will be published by the Patent Office as-is.

9 **UNDERGO A DETAILED EXAMINATION.** There is now a much more detailed examination of your invention, for which you have to pay another fee.

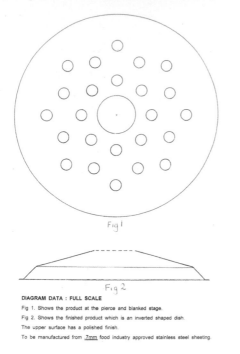

Fig 1

Fig 2

DIAGRAM DATA : FULL SCALE

Fig 1. Shows the product at the pierce and blanked stage.

Fig 2. Shows the finished product which is an inverted shaped dish.

The upper surface has a polished finish.

To be manufactured from .7mm food industry approved stainless steel sheeting.

RAYMOND SMITH FILED HIS DESIGN
(above, see also pp176–7) for the Magic Pizza with an EU Copyright Office at the same time as applying for a patent. Lodging a design with the office doesn't provide the same protection as a patent, but is a relatively easy interim measure whilst the patent process takes its long course.

10 **MAKE ANY NECESSARY AMENDMENTS.** The Examiner may require you to make amendments to your application after the detailed examination.

11 **HAVE YOUR PATENT GRANTED.** Once the Examiner is satisfied with the outcomes, your patent will finally be granted.

The process described above gives you full protection in the UK and streamlines the application process for obtaining rights for countries participating in the Patent Co-operation Treaty and the European Patent Convention.

COPYRIGHT PROTECTION

If your business produces something that takes a lot of effort but is not an invention as such, then your protection relies on copyright. You can't copyright the 'idea', but you can copyright the actual output based on that idea. For example, no one can copyright the 'idea' of a book, but the actual output of that idea (such as the book you are reading now) is copyrighted.

Copyright also covers pictures, software programs, designs, websites and theatrical work. Copyright lasts for the life of the creator plus 70 years in most cases of written work, and 50 years from production in the case of sound and broadcast.

Unlike patents, you don't have to register a copyright anywhere; copyright is automatic. However you are well advised to create an 'audit trail' in order to help prove that you own the copyright.

THE © SYMBOL

As a part of the 'audit trail', it is advisable to mark your work with the © symbol, followed by the name of the copyright owner (be it a personal name or the name of the business) and the year in which the work was created. This will let others know when copyright started and (in some cases, such as broadcasts or recordings) whether it has ended or not. It will also indicate who the owner is so they can ask permission to use your work. Make sure the name of the business rather than the name of a member of staff appears here. See also confidentiality and non competition on pp174–5.

WITH A BUSINESS VENTURE BASED ON AN INVENTION, *protecting the intellectual property rights to it is paramount. Michael Pritchard of Anyway Spray (above and see case study to right) had addressed this as a priority, and at the time of his appearance in the Den had already spent £100,000 lodging patent, design and registered trademark applications to cover markets in 48 countries.*

DATING THE WORK FOR COPYRIGHT

As another part of the 'audit trail', you could lodge your work with a bank or solicitor. Though this doesn't prove that the work is originally yours it does set the date you claim it as yours, which may become important if you ever need to take the matter to court.

There are some commercial companies offering an 'unofficial copyright register service'. If you are considering a service like this, look carefully at the cost/benefit ratio. Is it a one-off or annual fee? Does it provide any more proof of date or evidence of originality than the mailed copy or a copy lodged with a solicitor or bank? Does

ANYWAY SPRAY

Michael Pritchard's invention-based business featured on Dragons' Den in Series 7. His novel dip tube can be used in aerosols and trigger sprays – it features a special membrane enabling the spray to be used in any orientation and so can dispense every last drop of liquid. It also allows manufacturers to substitute the harmful VOCs used in aerosols with benign compressed air.

Michael's plan was to adopt an intellectual property licensing model, where companies would pay a royalty for using his patented technology in their spray products. The patenting process requires significant investment of time and money. Michael had not been awarded a granted patent at the time of filming, so, to some extent, the business was still a gamble to invest in. Peter and Theo, though, felt that it was worth the gamble over patents and, since Michael had at least followed the correct legal procedure and lodged them, they would be in a reasonably strong position with regard to any copycat products.

the service include legal insurance to fight a copyright case, which in itself may be adequate justification for use of the facility?

You could also send yourself a copy of the work by special delivery post (which gives a clear date stamp on the envelope), but you must remember to leave the package unopened to prove the date-to-content connection.

Note that neither registration nor sending a copy of the work to yourself show that you were the creator of the work. However, if you keep copies of all your drafts and research, this could be useful evidence if you ever have to prove that you are the originator.

TRADEMARKS

Whilst patents and copyright relate to tangible products (or certain processes), you can also protect your *image* with a trademark.

A trademark is the 'badge' that differentiates the products and services of one business from those of another. A trademark could be a word or title (including a personal name), letters or acronyms, numerals, logos or a permutation of any or all of these. It can be two- or three-dimensional and can even be a sound. The Intellectual Property Office manages all the trademarks in the UK.

You don't have to register your trademark, but it is highly recommended for the following reasons:

- Anything entered on the Trade Marks Register gives you the exclusive right to use the mark.

- It enables you to take legal action against anyone else who uses your trademark to their benefit.

- It enables the Authorities to bring criminal charges against counterfeiters.

- If you don't register your trademark, and another business starts using the same or a similar mark, you only have Common Law to rely on, which is tougher and more expensive to prove, as it requires lots of evidence that you have sufficient claim of ownership and that customers were under the impression they were buying your goods, rather than the infringer's.

- Registration gives you national protection even if you only do business locally. With an unregis- tered mark, you could find that you cannot stop a copycat business in another part of the country. Similarly, the copycat may be able to prevent you from expand- ing your business outside your initial locality.

- A registered trademark is legally your Intellectual Property, similar to having the deeds to a piece of land. A registered trademark therefore has a cash value – you can sell it or license it.

Note that registration of a trademark usually lasts for 10 years, then you have to pay another fee to renew it.

Before you try to register any trademark, you should carry out a search to check whether the mark you want (or anything very similar) is already registered. Doing a search could save you from an infringement action against you, stopping you using your own mark and leading to damages. Your intended trademark must be 'distinctive' and not conflict with any existing trademarks. 'Distinctive' normally rules out anything that is descriptive of the goods or services in question, common in your particular area of business, or that relate to some quality of the product.

A trademark is registered in relation to specific goods and services. This is made easier by the classification of all goods and services into 45 categories. It is likely that your need will cover more than one class, and the fee payable increases as the number of classes increases. Greater protection costs more money, so you need to think carefully about your current and future needs as well as affordability. You can download a document explaining the current fees and process from www.ipo.gov.uk.

The overall process for registering a trademark is similar to the process for a patent.

1 **APPLY FOR A TRADEMARK.** You submit an application form and a fee to the Intellectual Property Office.

2 **RECEIVE A CASE NUMBER.** The Intellectual Property Office sends you a receipt and a case number.

3 **WAIT FOR AN IPO REPORT.** The IPO examines your application, checks if it is similar to anything already registered, and sends a report.

4 **REVISE IF NECESSARY.** If the IPO has objections, you have the opportunity to argue your case and/or to make changes to your specifications or the relevant goods and services.

5 **HAVE YOUR APPLICATION PUBLISHED.** If they have no objections (or you have persuaded them that those objections are unfounded), then your application is published in the IPO's Trade Marks Journal.

6 **SEE IF ANYONE ELSE OPPOSES YOUR APPLICATION.** Anyone else now has two months to oppose your application (this can be extended to three months in some cases). If it is opposed the IPO will judge who 'wins' and the loser can be made to pay contributory costs (i.e. not all the costs but a contribution towards them; if anyone opposes your application it is going to cost you extra money, win or lose!)

7 **HAVE YOUR TRADEMARK REGISTERED.** If your application is unopposed, or you win the judgement over any opposition, your mark will become Registered and from then on you can use it and enforce your rights.

LOOKANDTASTE.COM, *the domain name for the venture of Niall Harbison and Sean Fee (see p207), was originally called ifoods.tv, but another website had virtually the same name – ifood.tv – so Niall and Sean wisely changed to a completely different name.*

MYDISH.COM *(Series 7) was chosen partly for the obvious comparison with myspace.com. The name immediately gives an accurate reflection of the site: a social network based around food.*

DIAMONDGEEZER.COM *– the domain chosen by Clive Billing (see p102) – gave rise to some discussion in the Den about negative connotations, but, as Clive pointed out, it is memorable and has the word 'diamond' in it.*

CREATING A DOMAIN NAME

A domain name is a name like 'coach-and-courses.com' (the author's own), which you use to direct people to your website and email. You do not have to be a company or organization to register a domain name. Any individual, such as a Sole Trader or even a private individual who wants a web presence can do it.

Having your own domain name gives your business credibility, and the name can be retained even if you change web host, which gives you continuity and makes it easier for your customers to find you. Another reason to create your own domain name is if you ever want to sell advertising space on your website – advertisers will take your site name into account, so a good, secure name raises your value.

Your domain name does not necessarily have to be your company name – you might prefer one that describes the business. For example www.diy.com is the domain name of B&Q.

If you look at the BBC domain name you will notice that whether you type in www.bbc.com or www.bbc.co.uk or www.bbc1.com you will always get to the BBC. This is because the BBC has registered names with different endings to 'protect' them from use by others.

By 2010 there were over 84 million domain names registered on the internet. Indeed, with many companies having bought up their names with various permutations – plus the activities of domain name traders (see next page) – coming up with something unique can pose quite a challenge to a start-up business. If the name you would like to use has already been bagged, you will have to think laterally, such as using a less common suffix such as .biz or .uk.com, or using 'the' or hyphens in the name, or a different name altogether.

It is worth noting that whilst the domain name is important for your business identity, it is not vital for Google and the other search engines, which are more interested in ranking the genuine content and metadata within a website rather than the website's name.

CHECKING DOMAIN NAME AVAILABILITY

If the domain name you want ends in .uk, you can use Nominet's 'WHOIS' service (at www.nic.uk) to check quickly for the availability or ownership of the name.

If the domain name you want has a different suffix, try typing the name into a browser's address line and see what comes up. If you get a simple browser message saying that the site cannot be found, then great – it's probably available, and you should be able to register it for a low fee (see below).

If when you type the address you want, however, you get a page of adverts with a message/link such as 'register this domain name', then you have a murkier situation. The name you want is held by a domain name trader or speculator, which may not necessarily be based in the UK. The price may then depend on a bidding system or by offer and negotiation. Some businesses have reluctantly paid thousands of pounds for the domain names they want.

REGISTERING A DOMAIN NAME

Some web hosts include registration in their cost, or you can use one of the many internet-based registrars. If you are using a registrar, check that it is accredited by the Internet Corporation for Assigned Names and Numbers (ICANN). The cost is variable but relatively low: £10 to £25 in most cases. Registration gives you the exclusive

BARBESKEW

Ed Wray's invention, the Barbe-
Skew, needed £180,000
investment when he visited the
Den. Ed demonstrated the product and the Dragons' verdict
was that it was a good idea and
product, and that the food
tasted great. So why did none
of them invest in the BarbeSkew?

THE BARBESKEW *is a cross between a
patio charcoal grill and a spit roaster: food
is put onto skewers, each of which rotates
automatically to make the cooking even.*

Well, Ed had looked into the
possibility of patenting his
invention, but found that it
wasn't possible because all the
individual elements of the
device had already been
patented – it was only the
combined use of them in a
barbecue that was new. He had
ownership of the trade name
BarbeSkew, but no real market
protection if a well-placed
competitor – such as a DIY
store, garden centre chain or
supermarket – decided to
launch a similar product.
If that were the case, Ed would
have to compete on price, and
that, the Dragons felt, would be
dangerous territory. This, combined with what was perceived
to be rather a high cost price
for the BarbeSkew, stopped the
Dragons from investing.

DESPITE NOT HAVING A PATENT *or Dragon investment for his BarbeSkew product (see previous page), Ed Wray has found enough of a market to progress his business.*

right to the name for a year; you must then renew it annually for a similarly low fee. If the fees are higher than this, then you are in the hands of a speculator (see previous section).

The important thing is to ensure that *you* rather than the web host are the owner of the domain name; otherwise you can find yourself suddenly being charged a potentially exorbitant fee to continue to use the name. When you register direct you can also ensure that you, not the web host, are listed as the technical and administrative contact. This means that you are in total control if, for example, you want to transfer to another web host.

CONFIDENTIALITY & NON-COMPETITION

If you are employing staff, sub-contractors, associates or business partners, you may well need to protect both your intellectual property rights and your relationships with your customers.

In practice this means having confidentiality clauses in contracts, stopping such people from using privileged information to your detriment, and having non-competition clauses to prevent them from poaching your customers.

Confidentiality clauses are relatively straightforward to include in agreements and contracts, and a quick web search will probably produce a range of options that are relevant to your area of business. Failing that, any trade associations should have appropriate recommendations.

Non-competition clauses preventing an individual or organization from working in the same industry sector after your relationship are difficult to enforce predominantly because they can be seen as 'restrictions of trade'. Non-solicitation clauses, which prevent the direct solicitation of your clients, are also difficult to enforce because they are easily circumvented – the ex-employee simply gets a colleague to make the call on their behalf.

In the right circumstances, however, such clauses working together can be effective, provided there is a legitimate business interest to protect and the clause goes no further than is necessary.

The courts are prepared to enforce such contracts where they accept that it requires all three to protect legitimate business interests. So, if you are setting up your business to compete with a previous employer… beware!

A 12-month restriction is considered to be the upper limit of what is acceptable for any restrictive covenant. The case of Thomas v Farr in March 2006 set a lot of the legal precedent in this instance.

It is advisable to seek proper legal advice on the wording of such contracts and clauses.

MAGIC PIZZA

Raymond Smith is a toolmaker by trade, with a passion for invention. Whilst working on a laser device for levelling snooker tables, he found himself eating a lot of frozen pizzas. And one thing he noticed was that the pizzas failed to cook evenly; they routinely had a 'soggy middle'. Raymond initially tried to combat this with the use of an upturned saucer, then an aluminium dome moulded on a saucer shape. It was a partial success, but still left a soggy underside to the pizza.

Raymond then embarked upon perfecting the invention, working with different sized holes and patterns to achieve the desired result. He phoned up one of the major UK suppliers of frozen pizzas to find out the

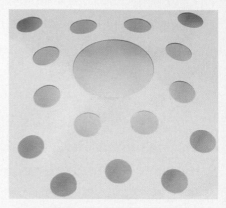

IT TOOK RAYMOND SEVERAL ATTEMPTS *to get the right combination of material, elevation and perforations in the metal disc.*

potential market for a product to nullify the 'soggy middle' effect, with the idea of supplying his Magic Pizza to the pizza producers.

On learning that 250 million frozen pizzas are sold annually in the UK, Raymond promptly decided to patent his invention. To get the ball rolling, he went to a patent agent in 2001 to work out the wording of the patent he would lodge. Over the following year, he amended this three times and also registered a Europe-wide copyright of the design to provide some fall-back position while the lengthy patent-granting process was taking its course.

The UK patent took about three years to be granted, and he had it secured well before venturing into the Dragons' Den – it was the saving grace of a nervy pitch. It seemed that none of the Dragons would be prepared to invest, until Peter seemed to surprise himself when he wondered if this could be the "cat's eye of the pizza world", after all. Deciding that, if it were, this would be too good an opportunity to pass, Peter made an offer for half the money for a 25% stake. It was then down to Theo to make or break the deal, and he decided that, for half the money, it was worth the risk.

THE MAGIC PIZZA *sits under the base dough and raises the centre of the pizza, enabling it to cook more thoroughly.*

RAYMOND FINALLY RAISES A SMILE, *having agreed a deal with Peter and Theo.*

COMMANDMENTS

SELL
SELL
SELL

Want to sell without
selling your soul?

MOST BRITISH PEOPLE dislike the idea of selling because they have a perception that selling is about snake oil promises, devious dealings and everything-to-the-salesman's-benefit. Entrepreneurs often try to kid themselves with the old saw that if they invent a better mousetrap the world will beat a path to their door. But this doesn't happen in the real world. Even if you don't consider selling to be your forte, you have to learn how to do it when you become an entrepreneur. You have to sell yourself along with your idea, and sell the thing itself to different people in different situations. In this chapter we show you how to do this part of your job intelligently and successfully.

Until a customer parts with cash for your product all you have in stock is liability. Until a customer pays you for your service you aren't paying the mortgage. You have to sell… or go out of business.

You have to get that 'Action' of AIDA (see Commandment 6) to happen, and to do that you need to get a couple of other things right:

- **YOU NEED TO UNDERSTAND YOUR CUSTOMERS**
- **YOU NEED TO GET THE BUYING DECISION**

UNDERSTANDING YOUR CUSTOMERS

There is no point in just knowing all about your product or service, no matter how cutting edge, innovative, lovely or brilliant you think it is. You must find out what the customer wants and needs first, then 'sell' what the customer will get out of your product or service.

In the world of selling, this concept is often referred to as 'Features and Benefits', and one way of getting the customer viewpoint is to engage in 'So What?' analysis:

"I bring 15 years' experience of working for the market leader."
SO WHAT?
"The customer can have big company expertise at a small company price."

"This product is made from space-age components."
SO WHAT?
"It won't break or need to be serviced; it is more reliable and cheaper in the long run."

"This invention is brand new."
SO WHAT?
"No one else has one so you will be a fashion setter."

"We sell everything you need for your project."
SO WHAT?
"One supplier means less procurement effort, simpler billing and volume discount."

You may get some understanding of your potential customers' wants and needs from your market research, but market research only researched the market, not the individual customer. You only find out what the individual customer really wants by talking with them.

MICHAEL LEA *appeared in Series 7, seeking investment for a mobile lunch service. In response to his customers' requests for afternoon ice creams, Michael devised a bespoke vehicle equipped with a refrigeration unit for his usual cold snacks and an ice cream machine for selling ices in the afternoons.*

THE WESTWOODS *and their Magic Whiteboard appeared in Series 6 (see pp228–9). Their pitch changed for the better when they were able to point out that the product was selling very well in Japan. Although the Dragons found it difficult to understand who the product was aimed at, they knew very well that the Japanese are early adopters of new technology and a good guide for future markets elsewhere.*

A 'hot button' in sales terms is the single criterion that convinces a prospective customer that they are going to buy your product. It may come from logic ("this service will save you money") or from emotion ("everyone else will be green with envy") or from following a recommendation ("fifty thousand other people can't be wrong"). You need to ask the customer questions to ascertain what will push their hot buttons.

THE DRAGONS' QUESTIONS INDICATE THEIR 'HOT BUTTONS'. *They are in the business of investment, so they want to know whether your company is going to make money for them – and how much. That's why they always ask about turnover, profit, debts, potential markets. Entrepreneurs often want to emphasize how good their product is – which is fine – but the ultimate decision will rest with the money questions. The Dragons have turned down perfectly good – even great – ideas and inventions in the past, and it is nearly always because they cannot see how they will make sufficient money from the business itself.*

Different customers want different things, so to sell to any one customer you have to fulfil their specific need. For example, some of your customers will be motivated by the third 'So What' example mentioned on the previous page – the idea of getting a brand new invention. In the IT world, such people are referred to as 'early adopters'. Whereas to more risk averse customers, 'brand new' means untested, untried, probably full of bugs or flash-in-the-pan.

Once you have got enough information about what this particular customer wants, then – and only then – can you tailor your 'sales presentation' or 'pitch' to fit their personal needs and wants. Here is where you 'sell' the benefits of your offering to the customer, so that you push their 'hot buttons'.

REACT TO BUYING SIGNALS

You may also have heard the term 'buying signal'. This is an expression of interest in a particular aspect of a product or service that gives you a hint of a customer's hot button.

Let's turn this on its head for a moment, and think of the last time *you* wanted to buy something. Whatever it was, you probably had some kind of mental list of things you wanted from the intended purchase. If it was a small everyday item you may have just done it intuitively in your head; if it was a big purchase you may have made a written list.

When buying or renting a home, for example, you might have a list such as: a separate study; good transport links; garden; quiet location. You look in the window of the local estate agent and see a nice-looking place, so you go in.

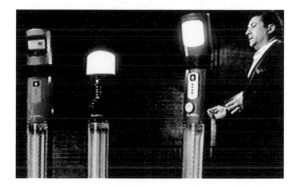

EDDIE MIDDLETON PITCHED *his patio heaters business, now known as Chillchaser, in Series 7. At least two Dragons – Peter and James – thought he had a good product. However, the entrepreneur did not sell the business well in his pitch, would not divulge important figures about the cost of manufacture and so lessened the strength of his negotiating position when it came to the point of a possible deal.*

The agent doesn't know what your list contains but asks if she can help you. You point to the property that's caught your eye and ask: "Is this close to the station?" You have just given the agent a buying

"IF YOU DON'T SELL, IT'S NOT THE PRODUCT THAT'S WRONG, IT'S YOU" ESTÉE LAUDER (1906–2004), COSMETICS COMPANY FOUNDER

signal – this tells her that transport links are important. Indeed, it being the first question you asked hints that it may be the most important criterion – the hot button. The agent now knows that there is no point in showing you properties that don't fulfil that criterion. Meanwhile, the property you've pointed at also happens to be in the catchment of a good school, so the estate agent asks if you have any children. She won't extol the virtues of the school until she knows the answer to that question. Not all prospective customers will have school-age children – to them the idea of being near the noise and traffic disruption of a school may be an active turn-off.

If you are selling to joint buyers (for example, life partners buying a car or business partners buying a piece of equipment), their individual hot buttons may be different: she wants a car that is a shiny soft-top sports car; he wants something big enough for his golf clubs. Push both hot buttons and you have a sale; push only one and you have a disappointment.

IDENTIFY THE END USER

Commercial buyers will similarly have lists of criteria to fulfil. The difference is that sometimes the buyer isn't the end user of the product and that makes a difference to your selling activity.

Sometimes it means the buyer is technologically more advanced than the user – IT departments for instance often procure for their organization's departments. Or the buyer is technically less savvy than the user – procurement departments may have a list of criteria from their organization but have little understanding of how it will work.

The buyer may have a completely different motivation from the end user. For example, the buyer for a retail chain will be interested in shelf-life, margin and your advertising – completely different criteria than those of the consumers who will buy in the shops.

Wherever you can, try to get access to the end user. That person has the real need and the hot buttons, whereas a buyer-on-behalf is likely to be less emotionally involved.

CLOSE THE SALE PROPERLY

For a customer to make a buying decision, the sale must be 'closed'… 'nearly sold' is not sold. A sale is said to be 'closed' when the customer actually signs on the dotted line or hands over the payment. Many sales opportunities (estimated to be about 60%!) don't get closed

MICHAEL NORTH PITCHED *for a members-only Olive Oil Club in Series 6 (see also p53). The upside of this approach is that, once you've made a sale (that is, enlisted a member for an annual fee), you will have effectively sold, in this case, 12 bottles of oil. The downside is that membership sales are that much harder to achieve. James felt the cost in marketing terms to attract enough people to the club would be prohibitively expensive and so couldn't see investment potential. The amount charged for each member would keep the business bubbling along, but wouldn't offer the returns needed for a business investment.*

SINCE APPEARING ON THE DEN, BUGGYBOOT *(left and case study, right) finalized their manufacture in the Far East and launched in summer 2009 through an exclusive agreement with a major high street chain (Mothercare). As their business builds, they are now selling via various independent and online stores and looking to increase their markets internationally.*

for the simple reason that the salesperson doesn't *ask* for the business. Asking isn't a matter of being pushy or pressurizing the customer; it is a matter of expediency. You won't get if you don't ask, so there is no harm in asking. There are several closing approaches for use in different circumstances and, yes, all of them can be used as high-pressure tactics, but they don't have to be used that way.

- **THE BASIC CLOSE:** "Would you like to buy?"

- **THE PRESUMPTIVE CLOSE:** "So, how many would you like?" or "When shall I start?"

- **THE EITHER/OR CLOSE:** "Would you like the red one or the blue one?" or "Do you want us to start next week or the week after?"

BUGGYBOOT

Charlotte Evans and Carolyn Jarvis asked for £80,000 in return for 10% equity when they visited the Dragons. Although they had worked on their Buggyboot project for three years and already invested £100,000, the business was still at an early stage.

They had good provisional orders, but what they required from a Dragon was not only money but also a strong business partner to help close the deals on the table and lead the way to new customers.

Dragon Deborah Meaden was keen to invest, though her offer was for a 30% stake rather than 10%. Charlotte and Carolyn had clearly expressed the potential for the product, but it was only that: potential. They therefore had to accept giving away 30% of the business. This was actually a good deal for them, but, having offered just 10% initially, they were unsure at the time, and hesitated before finally agreeing.

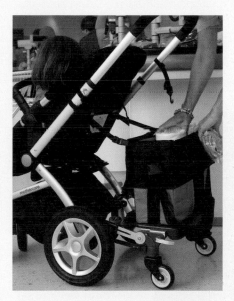

THE BUGGYBOOT *is a detachable bag that fits onto pushchairs and is positioned to aid stability and prevent tipping problems – a common occurrence when carrier bags are hooked onto pushchair handles.*

- **THE TESTIMONIAL CLOSE:** "Before you make up your mind, would you like to speak to XXX who bought one of these/uses our service, to get an unbiased opinion?" Surprisingly, this often encourages people to make up their mind there and then.

- **THE REVERSE PSYCHOLOGY CLOSE:** "I don't want you to rush a decision, so please think about it and I'll call next week – is Tuesday at 10 okay?" Surprisingly, this often also encourages people to make their mind up there and then. The important thing here is to make a specific time rather than just "Call me when you are ready."

The close(s) you choose to use may depend on the person you are selling to: consumer, retail buyer, commercial purchaser etc. There is a long list of possible closes at http://changingminds.org.

DRAGONS THEO PAPHITIS AND PETER JONES *shake hands with Jason Roberts of Tech 21 after agreeing a deal in Series 7. Jason had wanted £150,000 cash in return for 5% of Tech 21's business, but the Dragons felt the company was overvalued and negotiated a 40% stake in return for their investment.*

SELLING TO KEY ACCOUNTS

Received wisdom says that it is between four and seven times more expensive to win a new customer than to sell to an existing customer. Therefore, once you have a customer you should really make sure that you provide a service that keeps that customer loyal through their brand experience (see Commandment 6).

If your business is in the B2B marketplace you may well find yourself having to get on to a 'Preferred Supplier List' (PSL). For some businesses it can take several months of negotiations, presentations and submissions to get on a PSL and cost thousands of pounds. Once on a PSL, you have to make all the effort worthwhile and treat this client as a 'key account'.

However, beware of becoming too successful with any one key account. Two examples from the author's clients found that they were doing most of their turnover with one key account. In one case, the key account (a US-based multinational) filed for Chapter 11 bankruptcy protection, and the company's income dropped from £10.6 million to about £280k overnight. In the second case, the key account was taken over by a predatory competitor and the general outcome was the same.

Within a key account you need to ensure that you are maximizing your business by protecting it from both the competition who could be on the same PSL (they are seldom exclusive), as well as any change of personnel within the client. If you deal all the time with one person, what will happen if that person moves on? To do this you need to work on several areas, as shown over the next few pages.

1 **IDENTIFY WHAT YOU WANT TO GET OUT OF THIS RELATIONSHIP OVER THE NEXT 12 MONTHS.** This may seem like a no-brainer, but a key account might not necessarily be simply a 'nice little earner'. It could, for example, be a loss leader – you accept that this year you are unlikely to make a profit out of this client, but you are trying to use the relationship to build a reputation for the future. Or it could be the foundation of your business over the next year. One possible tactic is deliberately to get close to the client in the hope that they offer to buy your business – your exit strategy!

2 **IDENTIFY WHAT THE CLIENT IS TRYING TO ACHIEVE OVER THE NEXT 12 MONTHS.** This is the bit where you get in, and stay in, the loop of their business. This allows you to anticipate their needs and their problems so that you can propose solutions even before they raise them. Once you do this you move from 'preferred supplier' to 'partner', and that usually has greater longevity and is usually really profitable.

3 **CLASSIFY YOUR CONTACTS AT THE CLIENT.** You need to know who does what, who makes what decisions and what those people think of you. Classify all the contacts in the client company – are they friends, allies, neutrals, protestors or enemies? – and which of these people have influence over decisions. With this battleground analogy, plot people out onto a table like the one shown opposite.

Obviously if an influential person is an enemy, your interests are in jeopardy. If everyone is neutral, in No-Man's Land, the competition could easily undercut or undermine you.

PLOTTING THE CLIENT BATTLEGROUND

Players of unknown influence and allegiance

4 **DEVELOP A PLAN TO MANAGE THE ACCOUNT.** From these discoveries you can work out not only an operational plan to deliver what the client orders but also a plan to convert enemies into allies, keep friends happy, make friends of the neutrals and find out about players of unknown influence and allegiance. You can make a plan to anticipate changes in the client's business and to be ahead of the game; a plan to provide new services or products for the client that provide a benefit to them and a profitable business stream for you; and a plan to cross-sell into other parts of the client.

5 **THEN KEEP REVIEWING REALITY AGAINST THAT PLAN.** Revise the plan as necessary.

SELLING TO OTHER TYPES OF CUSTOMER

Where your existing customers are not 'accounts' as such, rather they are simply users of your product or service, you need to be consistently looking at ways to sell more to them. Two major ways of doing this are to sell them more of the same product/service, or to add other products and services that complement the original.

If you consider the former, probably the most famous example of selling more of the same product to existing customers is the shampoo instruction: "Wet hair, apply shampoo, massage, rinse *and repeat*"… potentially doubling sales overnight! To consider selling complementary services or products, you have only to look at your local golf club: they sell playing time on the golf course as their primary line of business but they also provide one-to-one coaching, junior classes (drawing in customers for the future), a shop selling accessories and equipment, a bar, a coffee shop and maybe an event venue for corporate and private events.

Where your business offering can sustain it, try to actively manage repeat sales. Here and on the next page are some general examples.

- **THE UPGRADE.** Software companies offer regular upgrades for a fee. 'Mark 2', 'v2.0' and '2nd Edition' are other examples of the upgrade approach to selling. Implicit in

"THERE IS ONLY ONE WAY... TO GET ANYBODY TO DO ANYTHING. AND THAT IS BY MAKING THE OTHER PERSON WANT TO DO IT. "

DALE CARNEGIE (1888–1955), AUTHOR OF
'HOW TO WIN FRIENDS AND INFLUENCE PEOPLE'

this approach is 'planned obsolescence'… the advertising strap-line of 'new and improved' is designed as much to appeal to the existing loyal customer to 'upgrade' as it is for the new customer.

- **THE SERVICE REMINDER.** Garages often diarize and send reminders to customers that their car is due to have its annual service. Dentists send out reminders of the six-monthly check-up.

- **THE ANNUAL MEMBERSHIP.** Institutes and associations usually require annual fees for members to remain registered. Some qualifications require annual renewal to prove up-to-date skills and knowledge.

- **THE TWO-FOR-ONE.** Supermarkets and large retail chains have made this selling tactic ubiquitous, but you must check your figures carefully to make sure your business can really pull off a promotion like this without going under.

- **THE LOYALTY CARD.** Offering discounts and freebies for repeat custom can be an effective tactic.

This Commandment is entitled 'Sell, Sell, Sell', and that is what you have to do. Make every day a sales day and every call a potential sales call. That doesn't mean being a sales bore – constantly talking about how great your product is – rather it means you have to become intensely interested in other people, constantly asking about their life/needs/business and listening to their answers. When you are working your socks off delivering a good service to your current month's orders, it is hard to motivate yourself to get up and make some sales calls. If you don't, though, you will suffer the stereotypical feast and famine of a start-up business. If you are able to keep making those sales calls as well as delivering ordered work, you are going to be successful and you are going to need to read Commandment 10!

RAPSTRAP

Andy Harsley had a great little invention when he went into the Den to ask for £150,000 investment in return for 15% equity. His Rapstrap – reusable plastic ties for use in bundling cables and wires, and packaging – was patented and had great market potential. So why was Andy happy to leave the Den with a deal that left him relinquishing a whopping 50% stake?

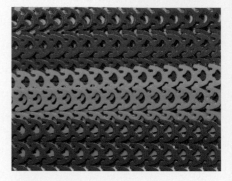

THE UNIQUE STRUCTURE OF THE RAPSTRAP *was patented by Andy.*

Well, Andy's primary research and development phase was over; he had a great product at a good price. The next stage was all about selling – getting his product out into the market as quickly and as widely as possible to recoup his investment and drive on the profit. All the Dragons showed interest in investing, but it was Duncan and James's offer that appealed most. Andy knew that they were already involved in businesses of a similar nature. To have two such Dragons on board would mean instant access to his targeted customer base in the UK and abroad. The cash would enable him to produce more in order to satisfy the demand that he was already struggling to meet (orders were being put on hold while Andy

released cash slowly for manufacturing); the Dragons would
help him penetrate the market
and make big-volume sales.

Indeed, you could say that
the selling had already started
in the Den. Andy had effectively
sold 50% of his business in
return for a cash injection and,
more importantly, the sales and
distribution network to launch
his business globally.

EACH TIE CAN BE WRAPPED AND TIGHTENED,
then cut short and the remainder used elsewhere,
making it a very cost-effective product.

IN THE DEN, THEO SOON SET ABOUT BREAKING A RAPSTRAP, *as is his want, but Andy*
kept cool and explained that cable ties don't need to be indestructible; they merely have
to be strong enough to hold cables together. Duncan ruminated on the Rapstrap, literally,
then he and James colluded on a deal. After wincing a little at the thought of giving
away 50% equity, Andy took them up on the offer.

COMMANDMENT 9

MAKE IT SHINE

Can you get ahead and stay ahead
of the competition?

YOU'VE DONE ALL YOUR MARKET RESEARCH, you've spent hours in intellectual deliberation, devising your strategy and tactics, you've crafted your plans and convinced yourself and everyone else involved of the way forward. Now you are in business. It is tempting simply to stick with the plan and go with it. Indeed it may be hard to find time to do anything else, but it is vital that you take some time each week to reflect and do some self-coaching. The business world is competitive – you need to react to feedback from your customers, fine-tune your product or service, strive for continuous quality improvement, and make yourself the best in your field.

There is a simple cycle, called the Deming Wheel, which sets out four steps in continuous quality improvement. (This is also often referred to as the PDCA cycle after the Plan, Do, Check and Act quadrants). You have already done the Plan bit… and your business activities, successful or unsuccessful, are the Do bit… so now you have to start on the Check bit…

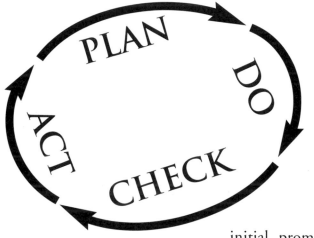

THE DEMING WHEEL, OR PDCA CYCLE

WHAT IS WORKING?

What are you doing that is working for you? Start with the initial promotional activity and assess whether it is getting the outcomes you wanted or planned for. Then look at the actual business you are winning – is it what you anticipated? Look at the margins – are you making the expected levels of profit from the specific pieces of business? What about your costs – are they in line with expectations? Then look at your operations and administration.

With regard to each of these elements, if the answers are Yes, ask yourself another question – could they be even better? 'Better' in this instance may mean a number of things: it could mean cheaper, less effort, more outcome. Remember that things don't have to be bad for you to want them to get better!

WHAT ISN'T WORKING?

What are you doing that *isn't* working for you? Again, start with the initial promotional activity and work your way through to the final admin and paperwork. When you are looking at what isn't working you need to assess why it isn't. You need to 'drill down' to find the actual problem. After all, you wouldn't want to throw away the car just because it had run out of petrol, would you?

Here is an example of how a business should actively seek out the real basic problem:

The owners of a start-up business created a website, expecting that this would attract enquiries for their services. They also engaged in direct marketing activity. For the first six months they worked hard to achieve their income targets and did so. At the six-month point it was noted that not one single enquiry had come from their website.

PARAGON PE WAS A YOUNG AND SUCCESSFUL COMPANY *selling high-specification cleaning products to the commercial sector. The owners had wanted to move into the domestic sector too and so launched a detergent called Halo, which featured in Series 7. Sales continued to grow fast in the commercial sector, but the domestic market was more sluggish and it was clear that to make a success of the Halo product would require more thought, time and effort. Rather than be distracted by this when there were clear profits to be made in the commercial market, they decided to concentrate on the expanding side of the business and renew their efforts on the domestic side once their brand had more presence.*

Their automatic assumption was that their customer base simply didn't search the internet when looking for suppliers, so they simply stopped updating their website as it seemed a pointless activity. Because they had a year-long web hosting contract, they left the current website in place.

At the end of the year, the business owners discovered that one of their newer competitors was generating so much web-originating business that they hardly had to undertake any other promotional activity at all. The team then discovered that their own website had experienced several thousand hits over the year, but people were not submitting enquiries. Further investigation showed that prospective customers were put off by the wording of the enquiry form, which sounded like they would be letting themselves in for a hard sell. The team rewrote the enquiry form and started to get enquiries within a matter of days. By the end of the year the website was generating more enquiries than they could handle along with their existing business, yet at a level which enabled them to expand the business… albeit six months late!

'DRILLING DOWN' QUESTIONS FROM THE PREVIOUS EXAMPLE

If you consider that example further, you can see how 'drilling down' requires a series of questioning levels.

"Are we getting prospect hits at our website?"

"Yes!"

"Do we get any enquiries from these hits?"

"No!"

"Do customers ever enquire via the web in this industry?"

"Yes!"

"Why therefore are we not getting enquiries?"

"Don't know!"

"Is it our prices?"

"Can't be, they aren't quoted!"

"Is it our products/ services?"

"Can't be, they are described in a similar way to our competitor's!"

"So what is it?"

"Don't know, let's ask some prospective customers!"

"What put you off making an enquiry on this website?"

"Well, your website asks for my budget along with my name, age, address and phone numbers – daytime, evening and mobile. Whereas your competitor's website asks simply what area I'm interested in and offers me a choice of an email response or a phone call."

Note that you couldn't discover this through a customer service questionnaire… each question follows on from the previous answer.

" BE A YARDSTICK OF QUALITY. SOME PEOPLE AREN'T USED TO AN ENVIRONMENT WHERE EXCELLENCE IS EXPECTED. " STEVE JOBS, APPLE CEO

LISTEN TO THE FOUR VOICES

When checking what is and isn't working, take time to listen to the four Voices: the Voice of the People, the Voice of the Process, the Voice of the Competition and the Voice of the Customer.

THE VOICE OF THE PEOPLE

This refers to the people who are doing the work, i.e. your staff and/or, in all probability, you! Ask whether they have the right skills, the right support, the right knowledge and, finally, whether they are happy. This last one may seem a little 'touchy-feely', but in a small business it is absolutely crucial. Consider yourself… you started this business for certain reasons of motivation; is it fulfilling your wants? Many people who start a business based on their hobby find that once their hobby becomes a 'have to do', it loses its charm.

Also take a check-up with the important people in your life. You may have roped your partner or spouse into the business in some way… is that still working?

Ask yourself and/or your people what else they need in order to do their job better. This could be tools, equipment, decision-making authority, access to you as the decision-maker, guidance or even freedom. Don't assume that because people aren't complaining that this means that they have everything they want or need. Create an appropriate environment of openness and ask them.

THE VOICE OF THE PROCESS

This refers to your work processes – the actual work itself and also all the processes that go before and after. For example, if your business is making and fitting bespoke household furnishings, the

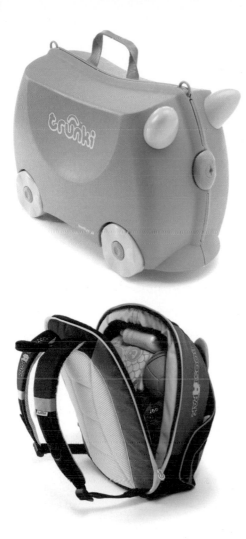

LISTENING TO THE VOICE OF THE PROCESS CAN HELP SAVE YOU MONEY.

One of the common ways in which companies reduce their outgoings is to move production to a cheaper part of the world where costs are lower. Jane Rafter of Slinks (see pp110–11), for example, had concluded that she could reduce her unit cost by a third by moving production to India, and Sammy French of Fit Fur Life (see p142) had her manufacturing in the Far East.

Each case is distinct, though, and with Trunki (see p225) a different approach was taken for the US market. One of the major stumbling blocks there was the 20% import duty on plastic luggage. After deliberating, Trunki concluded that the best policy would be to manufacture in the States rather than the Far East for that particular market. This got rid of the cost of shipping, exchange rate fluctuations and import duty. This is now something they've been investigating for the UK.

process may start with your initial advertising; the next step might be the prospect enquiry; then the site visit; the invitation to quote; then the 'survey'; next the commissioning; followed by manufacture; installation; sign-off; invoicing; then finally payment.

To listen to the Voice of the Process, draw it on paper, consider how long each step takes; assess the waiting between each step; look at the success of each step; and judge the acceptability of the cost of each step, including the delays. Look for ways to improve each step and therefore the process as a whole.

THE VOICE OF THE COMPETITION

You will have looked at what your competitors are doing before you started up your business. Now you yourself are up and running, you need to look again at what your competitors are doing, not just the ones you identified in your pre-launch research but also any new ones that have jumped on the bandwagon.

You might inadvertently be responsible for starting the bandwagon yourself when you're spotted entering the market. Others might perceive that there is definitely a market to be exploited and enter it themselves… or turn peripheral services into dedicated industries.

A real-life example of this is the estate agency business, which exploded in the early 1980s. Not only did new estate agencies spring up all over the place, but also existing legal firms and surveyors suddenly started offering property marketing services as a whole new line of business.

Look to see if any of the competition are trying to emulate your USP. If they are, then your USP isn't Unique any more, and you may need to rethink it!

NIALL AND SEAN'S REBRANDED LOOKANDTASTE WEBSITE *(above and right) launched in 2009. They have since also brought out an iPhone App to expand the versatility of the original concept.*

LOOK AND TASTE

It is tempting, when you have so much else going for your product and business, to overlook one flaw in the plan, assuming perhaps that the many positive factors will more than compensate for the single drawback. That's too much of a gamble, though, so tackle it before pitching for investment.

MICHELIN-STARRED CHEF *Niall Harbison and business partner Sean Fee made an enthusiastic pitch for their business.*

A case in point was Niall Harbison and Sean Fee's pitch for their food and recipe website iFoods.tv which featured in Series 6 of the Den. This was a great pitch by an acclaimed professional chef and his business partner, who had launched a website demonstrating recipes for viewers to follow. Everything was going extremely well with the pitch until the duo revealed that another site existed with an almost identical name, ifood.tv. Realizing that this would lead to confusion and website 'leakage' – people going to the wrong site – the Dragons wouldn't invest. Niall and Sean took on board the Dragons' advice and immediately after the show announced their intention to rebrand the site. They have since relaunched the site as lookandtaste.com.

"YOUR MOST UNHAPPY CUSTOMER ARE YOUR GREATEST SOURCE OF LEARNING " BILL GATES, MICROSOFT CHAIRMAN

THE VOICE OF THE CUSTOMER

Talk to all your customers to find out what you are doing right and what you could improve. Don't talk only to the 'nice' or profitable ones; talk to those who make your life a misery as well.

Talk too to the ones who nearly bought from you but didn't and the ones you pitched to but never heard from again. These are the people who can tell you how to win their business next time. This is not only good promotional activity (it gets you back in front of the customer), but is also a good way to find out what customers want (and often what your competitors are doing!) Ask your customers what you could do for them.

You can assess the Voice of the Customer by phone, email, face-to-face business meetings, social meetings or even by questionnaire – it depends on the number of customers you have and the type of business you are in.

THE MOMENTS OF TRUTH FOR YOUR CUSTOMERS

In Commandment 6 we discussed 'brand image'. Once your business is up and trading you have to be aware of the fact that the brand image is developed by the 'brand experience'. This is the impression of your brand gained by the marketplace, based on visual, verbal and experiential contact. You need to be very aware of what are called

YOU HAVE TO CONSTANTLY MONITOR AND REACT *to your customers' needs and habits. In a time of recession, sales fall directly as a consequence of people having less money to spend and also indirectly as other businesses – such as shops – go out of business. Youdoo (see p144) was facing just such difficulties around Christmas 2009. The problem was compounded by a weak pound, which effectively made the cost of manufacturing in China more expensive. The upside of a low pound, however, is that it makes selling into foreign markets that bit more attractive, and Youdoo plans to compensate for lower sales in the UK with increased sales abroad, particularly in the US, Japan and Australia.*

'Moments of Truth'. A moment of truth, or an MOT for short, is any interaction that a customer or prospective customer has with your brand, affecting their impression of the brand.

For some examples of the Moments of Truth, let's imagine you have a business that specializes in, say, designer bathrooms. Your business has a website, a person based in an office fielding phone calls and admin, and several people who go out to potential clients to measure up, design and install the bathrooms.

- **PHONE ENQUIRIES.** Every time someone calls the office they are having Moments of Truth. How long does the phone ring before it is answered? How is the phone answered? What is the message if the phone goes to voicemail? How long does it take to get a call back?

- **WEBSITE EXPERIENCE.** Every time someone hits your website they are having Moments of Truth. Do the designer bathroom pictures look genuinely stunning? Was the website easy to find from directories or search engines, and is there adequate contact information? Or is the website shot full of spelling and grammatical errors?

- **SIGHT OF THE COMPANY VEHICLES.** Every time someone sees one of your company vans, there are Moments of Truth. Does the vehicle look clean and professional, or filthy and battered? Is it driven courteously or does the driver cut people up? Is the tax disc up to date? Also bear in mind here that if the vehicle is a top-of-the-range Lexus, it may create a negative Moment of Truth by giving the impression you charge far too much!

MICHAEL LEA *of Earle's Direct proudly brought his mobile catering vehicle right into the Den in Series 7.*

- **IMPRESSION FROM APPEARANCE.** Every time someone sees one of your people in company branded work-wear they have Moments of Truth: does the way the clothes are worn look proud, smart and professional, or slovenly and unkempt? Is the person doing something 'dodgy' (e.g. peeing in the bushes, yelling down their mobile phone in an obviously aggressive way)?

Note that at this stage all these MOTs are happening before anyone judges the actual competence of your people!

- **IMPRESSION FROM INITIAL MEETING.** Obviously the prospect has MOTs when someone representing your company comes to look at a job and give a quote or estimate. Does the person quoting look as if they know what they are doing? Do they measure things and take notes or look as if they are making a wild guess?

- **WORKING PRACTICE.** Whilst the work is being done there are obvious MOTs as well. Do you and your people turn up on time? Do you only break appropriately? Is there a constant display of 'builder's bum'? Loud music? Mobile phone calls? Expletive language? Constantly having to go for more materials (which gives the impression of poor planning)?

" **NOBODY TALKS ABOUT ENTREPRENEUR- SHIP AS SURVIVAL, BUT THAT'S EXACTLY WHAT IT IS AND WHAT NURTURES CREATIVE THINKING. RUNNING THAT FIRST SHOP TAUGHT ME THAT BUSINESS IS NOT FINANCIAL SCIENCE. "**

ANITA RODDICK (1942–2007), FOUNDER OF THE BODY SHOP

- **FINISHING TOUCHES.** Even when the work is over, there are more MOTs. Is the site left appropriately clean and tidy? Has the job been done properly and on time?

- **DOCUMENTATION.** Finally, there are MOTs over the paperwork. Is certification provided? Are user guides handed over? Is the invoice as expected?

All these things create the brand experience on the visual and experiential levels. The verbal level – what people say about your business behind your back – is totally out of your control. All you can do is manage every single MOT to make it as positive as you can. Then you can ask the client to recommend you to their acquaintances if their experience has been satisfactory, or to give you a chance to put it right if their experience has been less than inspiring.

FINDING THE WAY FORWARD

Listening to all those voices is the initial part of the Check quadrant of the Deming Wheel. Go back to the beginning of this chapter if you've forgotten what that was. Next you need to decide what to do about the information you have gathered. (Sometimes this whole quadrant is referred to as Study).

You must carry out a cost/benefit analysis of any proposed changes to your business, paying particular attention to the 'downstream impact' of any changes you plan to make. Downstream impact is the effect that a change at any part of the process will have later on in the process. For instance, let's assume that you currently outsource your

printing to a local supplier but your People and Process Voices both suggest that this is costly, inconvenient and causes a delay. You want to buy a printer of your own so you can print on-demand. Downstream, however, you need to consider the space the printer will take up, the power it consumes, the heat it emits, the ink cartridges it uses, the service costs and the reliability.

If you discover that your USP isn't unique any more you are going to have to address this issue pretty quickly. You may be able to find an angle on the USP that restores its uniqueness, for example the 'original' approach may be adequate. You are more likely to have to seek out a new USP… this is going to mean starting all over again at the planning stage and really working on finding something that isn't so easy to copy.

Of course if you had a USP that was patentable or copyrightable in the first place, you should have secured it before you started, but most USPs for businesses rather than tangible products are not appropriate for this sort of protection.

CUDDLEDRY

Polly Marsh and Helen Wooldridge of Cuddledry appeared
in Series 5 of Dragons' Den
seeking investment in their
baby towel business. They
didn't secure a deal they could
accept in the Den, but since
then have had tremendous
success. They are very much an
object lesson in using feedback
from many sources to drive their
business forward.

CUSTOMER FEEDBACK *led to the inclusion
of hoods on the Cuddledry towels.*

The company has made use
of customer feedback and
retailer and trade feedback,
both on their products and the
way they do business.

As Polly explains, "It is very
important to us to make sure we
continue to give all our different
customers exactly what they
want – we want to make it as
easy as possible for them to

want to do business with us
above anyone else – of course!"

As a direct result of
consumer feedback, Helen and
Polly added a hood to the first
cuddledry towel, added a
whole range of new products,
expanded the age range to the
products and expanded the
markets they trade in. And they
switched from organic cotton to
a blend of organic cotton and
bamboo as a result of trade

feedback – a move that has also been popular with customers. They lowered their MOQs (minimum order quantities) for their trade customers too.

"How can we help you increase your sales? is basically what we ask," says Polly. "They tell us what they need, and we try to give it to them!"

The company also does special offers and added-value incentives, which its trade customers can pass on to customers or keep for themselves. As Polly says, "In this recession, it is important to allow our retailers the freedom to do whatever they feel they need to do in order to keep sales going – the small independents particularly. We provide trade customers with every single piece of marketing and promotional material we can – including press releases, images, video footage, stand display material,

HELEN WOOLDRIDGE AND POLLY MARSH *are the founders and co-directors of Cuddledry.*

point of sale leaflet and flyers – all to help them drive footfall into their shops and traffic to their websites."

CUDDLEDRY *has recently created an online trade website in order to give trade customers 24-hour online ordering capacity.*

GROW YOUR OWN

Can you handle the demands
of a sudden growth spurt?

BUSINESSES, like children, get growing pains. We have all heard of businesses and business people that were victims of their own success. Whether your business provides a product over the internet and your inbox is groaning with orders, or you provide a service and you simply cannot find enough hours in the day to visit and service all your clients, overnight success is not as 'nice' a situation to be in as you might otherwise have imagined. Sudden growth may be much better than having no orders, but it still presents major challenges that can be just as destructive as the latter if not handled well.

Your initial vision and business plan should consider your intentions as the business becomes established and grows at a pace you can control. That's the theory, anyway. In reality, planning for growth can be difficult. An understandable mindset that says "let's walk before we try to run" and sheer weight of matters prevent many entrepreneurs from doing much crystal-ball gazing about the future!

Anyhow, there are two positive situations that you may face when your business is up and running:

- **SCENARIO 1**

  You achieve your targets and your business grows steadily according to your plans. This gives you adequate time to make considered decisions about growth, expansion and resourcing your evolving business. Lucky you.

- **SCENARIO 2**

  You achieve a totally unexpected level of success in your sales activity and are rushed off your feet with orders. You are working all hours and constantly in demand. You find it difficult to find the time to stop and think about making deliberate plans for the future because you are just too busy keeping up with the demand for your time or product. Not so lucky you.

With Scenario 1 you have the time and the information to make careful and considered decisions, to take into account the opinions of relevant people and to weigh up the pros and cons of each option in a more deliberate way. With Scenario 2 you are under pressure

TONY EARNSHAW AND HIS COMPANY UKCC *appeared in Series 7. At that time his business was growing fast but steadily. The main base was in the Newcastle area and he had just opened a new depot in Leeds to spread operations across northern England. Tony has since developed a franchising arm of the business to service new contracts at a local level. Franchise operations are being set up throughout England, Scotland and Northern Ireland, and this growth strategy is intended to help UKCC increase its brand profile.*

both of urgency (you need to make decisions quickly in order to avoid disaster) and decision-making time (the actual pressure of delivering on existing orders is stopping you from taking the time to assess and analyse options). Consequently, it is a good idea to start planning for your success even before you start making sales. If you leave it until the sales are rolling in (i.e. you think to yourself "I'll cross that bridge when I come to it", or "that will be a great 'problem' to have" or even "I don't want to make a plan now that might jinx my chances of success"), you will make decisions in haste and be limited by short-term solutions.

So have a plan, ideally in writing. The rest of this chapter is aimed at getting you – as you start your business from a Zero base – to give some thought as to how you might handle great success, or to make quick decisions if you find yourself in this enviable situation!

THE SLATER 6S MODEL FOR DEALING WITH SUDDEN GREAT SUCCESS

Whether you are sitting down to plan this calmly in advance, or grabbing a half hour late on a Saturday night when the phone has finally gone quiet, you need to think through all the different aspects of expansion. To help you to think through all the relevant areas, there is the Slater 6S Model:

" A BUSINESS HAS TO BE INVOLVING, IT HAS TO BE FUN, AND IT HAS TO EXERCISE YOUR CREATIVE INSTINCTS. "

RICHARD BRANSON

So, let's say you have unexpected sales success. To exploit it and prevent it from causing your business to implode you need to have contingency plans for the six areas shown on the model.

SLATER 6S MODEL – SUPPORT AND STAFF

'Support and staff' can be regarded as one for the 6S model. If things get really busy and you and your existing staff cannot cope with it all, then who will support you? Can you call on family and friends to rally round? Who from previous employment would you offer work to? Will you employ more people permanently or on short-term contract? Can you get temps in to help and if so where will you find them? How do you pick people who will be of use immediately and possibly add value in the future? Do you use Associates? Do you sub-contract work out?

Also remember the aspects covered in Protect and Survive (pp174–5) concerning confidentiality and non-competition.

SLATER 6S MODEL – STRUCTURE

The structure of your business includes your management structure: the way you divide up different 'departments'. If you experience sudden growth, is your original structure going to be able to cope?

JOE READE'S ISLAND BAKERY ORGANICS
appeared in Series 7 with a proposal to expand its bakery. The expansion would enable the bakery to double its hourly output. Increases aren't all proportionate, however, and in order to double turnover, the company needed to increase output by a factor of six through additional shifts to make the expansion viable.

For example, do you have a far greater capacity for sales than you need and less than you anticipated for delivery of contracted work? If you are taking on new staff, who is going to manage them? And who is going to make sure they get paid? If you are going to sub-contract work out, then who is going to supervise the contractors? Is your finance function adequate to manage all the invoices and credit control? (Remember that the order is worthless until it is paid for.)

SLATER 6S MODEL – SUSTAINABILITY

There are three areas to consider here. Is the cost sustainable, is the activity sustainable, and is the demand sustainable?

- **COST:** Expansion is going to be required by the order book, but can you actually afford this expansion, today and in the future? You need cash in hand to pay for much of this growth activity, whilst you will also be committing future spending. For example, if you take extra space you

" AN ENTREPRENEUR TENDS TO BITE OFF A LITTLE MORE THAN HE CAN CHEW HOPING HE'LL QUICKLY LEARN HOW TO CHEW IT " ROY ASH, CO-FOUNDER OF LITTON INDUSTRIES

are committing to rent; if you employ people you are committing to salaries; if you borrow money you are committing to interest payments. You are probably going to need to find a source of funds, whether by borrowing or selling part of your investment.

- **ACTIVITY:** Can you sustain the activity required to meet demand? If you rope in friends, for how long will they support you happily? If you employ temps are they available year round or is it a seasonal availability (university holidays for example)? What is their turnover rate and how much time do you need to train them?

- **DEMAND:** Is this level of demand likely to continue or have you hit a seasonal rush or fashion fad? Can you keep up the sales activity whilst struggling to deliver what has already been sold? This is the most common problem for many small businesses; it results in a 'feast and famine' cycle that causes so much stress and heartache. Should you consider licensing or franchising as a way of overcoming this problem?

SLATER 6S MODEL – SYSTEMS

Love them or hate them, we are all reliant on computers nowadays. Have you got enough of them to cope with your growth? Do they talk to each other? Is it time to get some form of ERP (Enterprise Resource Package) that will automatically convert an order into job card, a job card into a material request, a material request into a purchase, a completion into a despatch, and a despatch into an invoice?

'Systems' also includes non-computer items such as your switchboard or phone system. Is the switchboard adequate for the number of extensions you need? Is the cabling in place? Are there enough handsets to go round all these new staff? Is there a system for people to quickly get what they need in order to provide customers with service? For instance, does anyone else have signing power over cheques, or a company credit card to go and buy material and equipment? Are your distribution systems adequate or do you need to outsource operations? See the case study on Trunki to see how one company's systems had to alter with sudden growth.

WISELY, ROB AND THE TRUNKI TEAM *(see opposite) have spent a lot of time with their business partners and chose them carefully so they knew they could work together to help grow the brand. In their case, distributors had the right resources and motivation to help market Trunki, whereas they themselves didn't have the resources to distribute internationally and the agents they had previously dealt with were less committed to the long-term project.*

TRUNKI

New markets came surprisingly quickly to Trunki's founder, Rob Law, who went into the Den in Series 3. He'd been a big fan of design blogs and used them to introduce his product. Within hours of sending information to blogs, positive reviews were being posted. The company's web traffic went off the charts. Rob even received an email from the Museum of Modern Art in New York, and they became Trunki's first overseas customer. Rob also had enquiries from Japan, Australia and France, and it all became overwhelming.

Rob got some great advice from the UKTI (UK Trade & Investment) who run a 'Passport for Export' scheme,

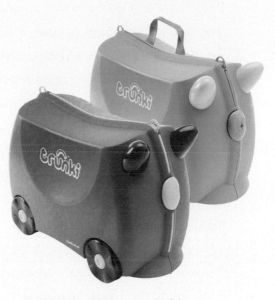

THE ORIGINAL TRUNKI *is a playful suitcase designed for children.*

encouraging British businesses to export. This involved a two-day training course where Rob gained valuable advice on everything from export strategies to funding overseas trade fairs. Rob decided to use distributors as a means of entering new markets. He now has about 16 distributors building the Trunki brand in dozens of countries.

SLATER 6S MODEL – SPACE

Where are you going to find appropriate space for the expansion? If you've been using your home for your business, you don't want to have to pile valuable sold stock in the damp shed, and you don't want to put the new finance department in the kitchen. If you already have business premises, is there a way of expanding in the near vicinity? You probably can't annexe the pavement outside for your increased delivery fleet! Do you need a completely different location with better transport links? The stakes rise with every upgrade.

SLATER 6S MODEL – SOCIAL

Finally, think back to your original motivation for setting up this business. If you set out to become a future captain of industry then you should have been planning these things already. If you set up a business to drop out of the wage-slave market, you need to be assessing the effect this is going to have on your health, family and sanity. Is now the time to activate Exit Strategy A?

> " **OFTEN THE DIFFERENCE BETWEEN A SUCCESSFUL PERSON AND A FAILURE IS NOT ONE HAS BETTER ABILITIES OR IDEAS, BUT THE COURAGE THAT ONE HAS TO BET ON ONE'S IDEAS, TO TAKE A CALCULATED RISK – AND TO ACT** "

ANDRÉ MALRAUX (1901–76), FRENCH WRITER

NEIL WESTWOOD OF MAGIC WHITEBOARD *(see pp228–9) moved out of his home business into an industrial unit as his company was growing so rapidly: "We started off with the Magic Whiteboard but the black version has proved even more versatile. More than half our sales will be for the baby market and the Magic Blackout Blind. The police have also started to use the Magic Blackout Blind to blackout windows at crime scenes. Schools are also buying the Magic Blackout Blind for classrooms so they can see the interactive whiteboard better."*

Getting to the point where these questions are in need of serious answers is great – it means you're successful! Your start-up business is a start-up no longer; it is now a fully-fledged enterprise. But you need to understand that this is the point where many businesses stall, stutter, crash and burn. The very skills and attributes of the founders that made the business a success now stop it from exploiting its opportunities. The ability to manage a larger business is often very different to the entrepreneurial drive to create something from nothing, to go from Zero to Business Hero. We recommend that you now read *Dragons' Den: Grow Your Business* to help you make the transition from Business Hero to Business Legend!

MAGIC WHITEBOARD

Neil and Laura Westwood presented the Magic Whiteboard to the Dragons in Series 6. As pitches go, it was a slow burner, with the Dragons struggling to find much excitement in a roll of statically charged white plastic sheet, which can be torn off in sections and used as an alternative to a flip chart. Peter Jones in particular couldn't see the point of it, and wondered why there needed to be an alternative to a standard whiteboard or flip chart.

However, the Westwoods gradually revealed the potential market for the Magic Whiteboard, and interest grew markedly after the disclosure that 200,000 units were being

NEIL AND LAURA *exchange a glance of approval before accepting investment from Theo and Deborah.*

sold annually in Japan, which is generally seen as an 'early adopter market'.

With a high mark-up between cost and retail price, exclusive distribution and selling rights to the UK and Ireland already in place, and profits forecast at £1.4 million within three years, the Westwoods eventually snared two Dragons, Deborah Meaden and Theo Paphitis.

Since their appearance on the Den, the business has grown rapidly – even faster than forecast – expanding from a small home business, in which they were posting out the products themselves each week, to a business with a national presence. Their online sales have grown and, with the help of the Dragons, they have ventured successfully into the major stationery and office suppliers throughout the UK.

THE WESTWOODS *envisaged the Magic Whiteboard as a product for corporate and educational use in lectures and presentations. Customers soon found many more uses for it though, such as for childrens' craft activities (as below). Their Magic Blackboard also began to be used as a blackout material, leading to a further product tailored to this use.*

The business has had to react fast to unexpected new markets too, such as children's playgroups and schools (see p227). They hadn't foreseen the product's use in the education sector, but in response they have taken the Magic Whiteboard to educational trade fairs and developed new products – such as a blackboard version that can be used with chalk and magic markers – aimed at these emerging markets.

DOS AND DON'TS

1 **DO BE 100% COMMITTED.** Starting up a business can't be a half-hearted affair. You need loads of time, passion and energy, and possibly the support of your family. Be clear about your motivation and exit strategy from the outset.

2 **DO RESEARCH YOUR MARKET.** Every new business needs a unique selling point in a competitive business world. You must first thoroughly research the market for your product or service, then decide how to position your offering.

3 **DON'T UNDERESTIMATE THE PAPERWORK.** Dealing with legal documents, VAT returns, liability insurances, employer's obligations and health and safety issues are part and parcel of a business owner's daily life.

4 **DO WRITE A DETAILED BUSINESS PLAN.** There is no better way to focus your thoughts than to commit your plan to paper, and your bank manager and investors will expect to see a professional-looking business plan.

5 **DON'T OVERLOOK ANY AREAS OF SPENDING.** Underestimating costs is a major mistake of many entrepreneurs. Make sensible calculations about how much money you need to start up before you approach any lenders or investors, or commit too much of your own money.

6 **DO EXPLORE BRANDING AND PROMOTIONAL ACTIVITIES.**
Create a strong, clear identity for your products or
services, and work out how to appeal to the kind of
customers you want from the outset.

7 **DON'T LET COPYCATS RUIN YOUR BUSINESS.** The
patenting process is long drawn-out, complicated and
costly, but it might be prudent for your business. Applying
for trademarks, using copyright protection and bagging
certain domain names can also help with protection.

8 **DON'T SHY AWAY FROM SELLING.** Even if selling doesn't
come naturally, you must get out there and sell yourself
and your business using tried and tested sales tactics.

9 **DO STRIVE TO STAY AHEAD OF THE GAME.** The business
world is in a constant state of flux, so you must monitor
your competitors and keep reacting to customer feedback
in order to stay ahead.

10 **DO PLAN FOR GROWTH.** All entrepreneurs hope for
success, but they should also understand that rapid
expansion can be one of the greatest risks for a business.
Make plans now for how you will manage people and
resources if your business really takes off.

JARGON BUSTER

AIDA
Acronym for Awareness, Interest, Desire, Action – the four stages of the promotional cycle.

ASSETS
Money, equipment and other valuables owned by a business.

CAPITAL
Broadly, financial assets.

CASH FLOW
The movement of money in and out of a business over a given period.

CREDIT
Broadly, receiving goods or services in advance of payment.

DIRECT COSTS
Costs directly related to providing goods or a service, e.g. production costs. Compare with indirect costs.

EQUITY
Portion of a company's assets owned by shareholders: equal to total assets minus liabilities.

FINANCE
Raising money through debt or selling equity. More broadly, the management of money.

FIXED COSTS
Costs that remain fixed even if production levels change, e.g. rent, business rates.

HMRC
Her Majesty's Revenue and Customs – the UK tax collectors.

INDIRECT COSTS
Costs not directly related to providing goods or a service, e.g. maintenance and security. Often they are fixed costs and part of overheads.

IPO

Intellectual Property Office.

KEY ACCOUNT

A very important client.

LEAD TIME

Time for an operation to be completed, e.g. from placing of an order to receipt and payment.

LIABILITIES

A business's debts and other potential losses.

LIMITED COMPANY

Popular business structure that gives its owners limited liability.

LIQUIDATION

Selling all of a company's assets in order to pay back debts and then distribute the remaining funds to shareholders.

OPERATING EXPENSES / OVERHEADS

Day-to-day costs of running a business, such as administration, as opposed to production costs.

PATENT

The exclusive right to make use of an invention or process in a country for a specified time.

PDCA CYCLE / DEMING WHEEL

Plan, Do, Check, Act – the quality control cycle.

SOLE TRADER

A business entity owned and run by one individual.

TRADEMARK ™

Right to exclusive use of a logo or word for your image.

USP / UNIQUE SELLING POINT

Your defining position in the market.

CREDITS

Produced by Thameside Media
www.thamesidemedia.com

Creative Director & Photographer: Michael Ellis
Editorial Director: Rosalyn Ellis
Assistant Photographer: Sergio Zimerman
Proofreader & Indexer: Zoe Ross

DRAGONS' DEN

Dragons' Den and all associated logos, images
and trade marks are owned and/or controlled
by 2waytraffic, a Sony Entertainment
company/CPT Holdings

Product Director: Lisa O'Connell
Licensing Director: David Christopher

The publishers would like to thank Sam Lewens,
Holly Simpson, Helen Bullough and Richard
Curwen at the BBC and all the Dragons' Den
entrepreneurs who kindly provided assistanc:

Michael Pritchard of Anyway Spray; Ed Wray at
BarbeSkew; Richard Enion and Michael Davis of
BassToneSlap; Frank Drewett of Bin Lid Lifter;
Simeone Salik, Janice Dalton and Dominic
Lawrence of Blinds In A Box; Charlotte Evans and
Carolyn Jarvis of Buggyboot; Helen Wooldridge
and Polly Marsh of Cuddledry; Michael Cotton of
DDN; Clive Billing of Diamond Geezer; Michael
Lea of Earle's Direct; Eglu; Sammy French of Fit
Fur Life; Laban Roomes of Goldgenie; Peter Neath
and Ian Worton of Grillstream; Joe Reade at Island
Bakery Organics; Karen O'Neill and Karen Coombes
of KCO Iceblading; Raymond Smith of Magic
Pizza; Neil Westwood at Magic Whiteboard; Sharon
Wright of Magnamole; David and Patti Bailey of
Motormouse; Victoria McGrane of Neurotica;
Michael North, The Olive Man; Paul Ward of
Paragon PE; Kay Russell of Physicool; Andy Harsley
of Rapstrap; Red Button Design; Max McMurdo of
Reestore; Toby and Oliver Richmond of Servicing
Stop; Samantha Fountain of Shewee; Lesley-Ann
Simmons of Shoes Galore; Jane Rafter of Slinks;
Ronan McCarthy of Spit 'n' Polish Shoeshine;
Shaun Pulfrey of Tangle Teezer; Rachel Watkyn of
Tiny Box Company; Steve Smith of trueCall; Rob
Law at Trunki; Sarah Lu of Youdoodoll; Tony
Earnshaw of UK Commercial Cleaning

For the official Dragons' Den website, see
www.bbc.co.uk/dragonsden

PICTURE CREDITS

Thameside Media: jacket photography and
opener images of the Dragons' Den; studio
photography pp18, 38, 70, 95, 170, 191, 200,
220, 227 (modelled by Minna and Marlowe Ellis)

Images of entrepreneurs' products and premises
kindly supplied by the businesses named

Evan Davis, p10, provided by HarperCollins

Shutterstock: pp 62, 65, 73, 77, 78, 81, 85, 86,
93, 105, 108, 125, 126, 128, 129, 131, 148, 149,
158, 163, 167, 188, 193, 195, 202, 210, 213

ALSO IN THIS SERIES

Dragons' Den: The Perfect Pitch
(Collins, 2010) ISBN 978-0007364275

Dragons' Den: Grow Your Business
(Collins, 2010) ISBN 978-0007364268

FURTHER READING

For business coaching, see the author's website at
www.coach-and-courses.com

Dragons' Den: Success, From Pitch To Profit
(Collins, 2008) ISBN 978-0007270828

Duncan Bannatyne *Anyone Can Do It: My Story*
(Orion, 2007) ISBN 978-0752881898

Duncan Bannatyne *Wake Up and Change Your
Life* (Orion, 2009) ISBN 978-0752882871

Duncan Bannatyne *How to Be Smart with Your
Time* (Orion, 2010) ISBN 978-1409112884

Duncan Bannatyne *How to Be Smart with Your
Money* (Orion, 2009) ISBN 978-1409112860

James Caan *The Real Deal* (Virgin, 2009)
ISBN 978-0753515099

Peter Jones *Tycoon* (Hodder, 2008)
ISBN 978-0340952351

Deborah Meaden *Common Sense Rules* (Random
House, 2010) ISBN 978-1847940278

Theo Paphitis *Enter the Dragon* (Orion, 2009)
ISBN 978-0752894225

INDEX

"I've got a great idea . . . a helicopter ejector seat!"

Are you in or out?

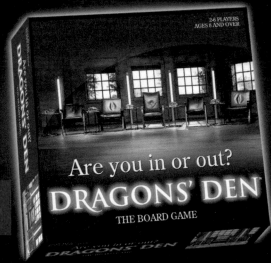

- You are a Dragon. Can you tell the brilliant from the bonkers?

- Would you invest in a man called King Camp, or risk it all on a frog wrapped in foil?

- What went Boom and what went B It's time for you to find the goldmine the official Dragons Den™ Boardgan

20%OFF! AND FREE P&P
at Winningmoves.co.uk/sh

DRAGONS' DEN™
THE BOARD GAME